IT AIN'T ALL GLITZ & GLAMOUR!

Byron Gibson

First published in paperback by Leap Street Publishing in 2024.

Copyright © 2024 Byron Gibson

Byron Gibson has asserted the right to be identified as the author of this work in accordance with the Copyright, Designs and Patents Act 1988.

All rights reserved.

ISBN; 978-1-80517-472-1

No part of this publication may be reproduced, stored in a retrieval system, or transmitted, in any form or by any means, electronic, mechanical, photocopying, recording or otherwise, without prior permission of the publishers.

Cover design by Taffy Edwards

CONTENTS

Take 1: Sounds Rolling & Action...1
Take 2: Smash It!..27
Take 3: Trench Foot & Ring Worm 41
Take 4: All Aboard The Piss Boat 56
Take 5: Time For Action..73
Take 6: Aim at the Target & Fire 89
Take 7: Gangsters Paradise...102
Take 8: No Budget No Problem!..135
Take 9: Intensive Care!..146
Take 10: Backstabbers 171
Take 11: The Con is On! 187
The Last Take 257
Disclaimer...269

ACKNOWLEDGEMENTS

I would like to express my sincere love and gratitude to Leigh for her unwavering support throughout this journey. It has been one crazy ride. To all the esteemed producers, directors, casting directors, actors, stunt coordinators and film crews who have placed their confidence in me during my career in film, I extend my utmost respect and affection to you all. Even to those who may have been less than reputable, I extend my appreciation, for without the experiences I gained while working with you, I would not have been able to write this book. As for those with ambition, I encourage you to pursue it vigorously and not let anyone discourage you. While you may perceive my journey as nearing its end, I assure you that I am only just beginning.

Byron Gibson, 2024.

This book is a memoir. It reflects the author's present recollections of experiences over time. Some names and characteristics have been changed, some events have been compressed and some dialogue has been recreated.

PINS AND NEEDLES

This scene is as sharp as the torturer's weapons of choice. Women are told to close their eyes and it's all we can do to keep ours open! Chang's looking to find out who ordered the hit on him and Byron's got answers. Nailed to the chair he sits in, first through his arms and then through his thighs, Byron might believe the worst was over, but no! A symbolic removal of the eyes is followed by a skewering of the eardrums and for us, a considerable turning of the stomach!

The character mentioned in that paragraph was me. This was from Watch Mojo's Top Ten Torture Scenes. The scene came in at number nine, just after *Braveheart* and was from the film, *Only God Forgives*, released in August 2013. The film caused much controversy at the Cannes Film Festival due to this horrific torture scene. There were boos and there were walk-outs from the critical elite. However, despite the outcry, I relished every minute of it. Ten years later, I'm happy to share this book with you. I hope that you will gain some knowledge about the wild world of the movie industry.

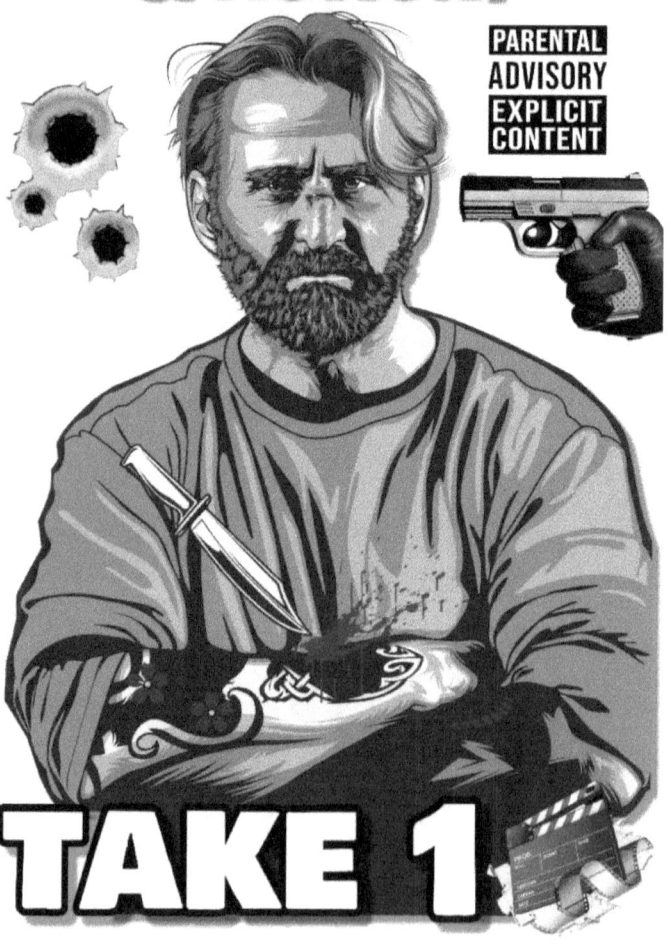

TAKE 1

My name is Byron and I have made an honest living by portraying the bad guy in films and TV productions since 2008. I am certainly not a celebrity, role model, or claim to be. You may have seen me in the movies being mutilated, shot, or having a horrific ending. I have played the antagonist in over seventy productions worldwide. It's been a hell of a ride and it's still not over. Many actors portray the protagonist and have written books about their acting journey. I'll give you an alternative perspective on the movie industry. Without us baddies, these movies wouldn't exist. The more successful the villain, the more successful the picture. As kids, we loved heroes, as adults, we understand the bad guys. Movie villains are some of the most important characters in any flick, having an antagonist who creates conflict for the main character can be integral to a film's plot. Every story needs to feature a scoundrel or a group of wicked characters because the hero can't shine without them. We are the unsung heroes.

To all you armchair critics out there, listen up. When I entered the film business, I was 38 years old. Some may say, "You're too late in the day for that and you won't get anywhere with it!" This book will prove these types of people wrong. With a positive mindset, there is always time to start anything. You can achieve anything within reason if you have the willpower and drive! The world is your oyster if you're fit and healthy! We live on a fascinating planet. Enjoy the day, set goals and don't feel sorry for yourself. We only live once and we are long dead. Failure doesn't have to be fatal, it can be an opportunity to learn. Whether you win or lose, go for it. You may have wondered if I've always worked in the film industry and the answer is no! I have always earned a living the arduous way, grafting and hustling. I wasn't born with a silver spoon in my mouth. My primary background is construction. I have worked in factories and workshops and done various jobs to earn a crust. I've always been an entrepreneur. I am proud to be a champion Thai boxing trainer and promoter. Several of my gym's fighters fought in the United States, Australia and Europe. I promoted Thai boxing shows for the first time in Cambridge, England in the early 1990s. During the MMA explosion, I introduced one of the first British fighters to bare-knuckle combat in a four-metre cage in Brescia, Italy. After establishing myself over the years and achieving success, I was ready to take on another challenge.

I wanted to explore other opportunities and push my own boundaries, so I decided to pursue a different path. I took some time out and went travelling. Around 2001, I set up market stalls selling gear I imported from Thailand. My stalls were around London and East Anglia. Working on a market stall is one of the finest ways to learn the craft of acting. I used to do a stall opposite McDonald's in Bury St. Edmunds on Saturdays. It was like a masterclass in improv.

I had to think quickly on my feet and come up with creative solutions to spark people's interest. I also had to convince them to part with their money. There was a stall next to me selling rheumatoid arthritis bangles. The stall owner was a guy named Rod, who was a genuine wheeler dealer and opportunist. He bought the bangles for a quid from the local Poundland shop just outside the town centre. He would put them in an elegant box and sell them for a tenner on his stall! Rod made a killing. Although dishonest, he was a kind chap and a lovable rogue. Rod was in his mid-sixties and looked like a gangster. He even wore a Fedora Trilby, just like Al Capone. From the streets of Hoxton, he carried the grit and grime of the East End in his every step. His voice, rough like sandpaper, held the echo of countless bargains struck and deals done. But beneath the gruff exterior, there was a warmth and loyalty that shone through in his smile, a flicker of humanity from the concrete jungle. Apparently, he knew Jason Statham back in the day when he did Great Yarmouth markets. Unfortunately, Rod died of a heart attack a few years later. Rod and a few other colourful characters have always stayed in my mind and have greatly influenced my acting style.

So, as you can see I have many strings to my bow and have used them in my career over the years. It may seem unorthodox to some of you, but I am not a trained actor. I've drawn on my life experiences and put them into action in my acting. Twenty years ago, if you had told me I would be in the film industry now, I would have laughed at you. I wasn't the slightest bit interested back then. I am an average working-class guy who fell into acting by accident, being in the right place at the right time, capitalising on that experience and falling in love with it. A warning to all you actors out there, some unscrupulous individuals are watching you. Always be on good behaviour. Everybody knows everybody in the film business. Now I will take you on a relentless journey of ambition, 5899 miles from my hometown, where it all began in Thailand, the Land of the Smiles. You're going to love it!

I relocated to Bangkok with my partner Leigh in 2006 after almost 16 years of frequent travel there. I got pissed off with the daily grind of living in England and wanted more from life. I first flew to Thailand to train in a passion of mine, Muay Thai, in the early 1990s.

Since that first visit, it was my dream to live in Thailand. It offers delicious food, a warm climate, cheap living, beautiful beaches and pleasant people! We lived in an apartment complex off Pratunam near the city centre for the first few years. One of the tallest buildings in Bangkok is the Bayok 2 Tower, which shadows the city and looks like a giant lighthouse. The iconic tower is 304 metres tall and looks stunning at night. We lived five minutes away. Anyone familiar with the area knows where I am talking about. It's just off Ratchaprarop Road. You cannot miss it! Many bizarre things occurred there. The apartment complex had over 500 rooms on 23 floors. It was one of the most polluted areas of the city. The building had a large community of colourful people, ranging from families, nurses, office workers, hookers, ladyboys, porn stars, ex-pats, gangsters and friends I still keep. The apartment complex was like a microcosm, a diverse and vibrant melting pot of different cultures, lifestyles and individuals all living under one roof. It wasn't a boring place to live, as you can imagine. Something was always brewing! There is so much to say about that place that I have written a book about it called The Bangkok Mansion. A book that'll leave your pulse hammering long after the last page. I ran an export company shipping retail and wholesale goods to the UK, which I set up off the back of my market business. I would buy the goods from Chinatown for 50 pence and sell them in the UK for a tenner, a tad better than my mate Rod! There was hardly any competition back then and the business thrived. I had an extensive database of customers who bought from me regularly. Honestly, I didn't want for much and I lived the life of Riley. Then, one day, I had a chance encounter with a well-known former Californian prison inmate who influenced me in my career.

I ate lunch with my partner Leigh at an excellent restaurant down an avenue called Soi Rangnam. The restaurant was called Seasonings and it was one of our favourites. It wasn't a glamorous place, but it served traditional Thai food and it was popular with locals. During our meal, we caught a mean-looking Mexican guy staring at us from across the room. The man had a big moustache, muscles, tattoos and he appeared very familiar to me. We were the only foreigners in the restaurant and there was lots of eyeballing. After a few minutes, we finally smiled at each other and broke the ice. The intimidating Mexican guy introduced himself as Danny Trejo. I thought I knew him from somewhere, but I couldn't work out from where until he explained to us that he was an actor. Then I realised who he was. He asked what we were doing in

Thailand. Leigh said she was working on a movie called *Shanghai* and choreographing the dancers. Her experiences in the industry interested him and he encouraged her to continue working hard. Danny asked me what I was doing in Bangkok for a job and I replied, "I'm not in the film industry, just running an export business nothing glamorous."

Danny told us about his remarkable life. He spent time in some of the most notorious prisons in America. His film career began in 1985, when he accidentally landed a part in the American indie film *Runaway Train.* In this film, Danny played a boxer. After that, he starred in films, including *Desperado, From Dusk Till Dawn* and hundreds more. He said he put his life experiences into his character roles. I loved it because this guy was down to earth and had no ego. He gave us some very valuable advice that day. He stated, "You need to get your face seen and do every job possible, from extra to featured extra to main roles if you're starting out, even if they pay peanuts. Sooner or later, someone will recognise you and your work ethic will start landing you character roles."

I thought that advice was golden for anyone trying to get into the industry. We sat there chatting for ages and then Danny had to leave to work on set. That was the last time I saw him. Little did I know how valuable that advice would be to me in the near future. Within three weeks of that chance meeting, I was about to start an exciting career with one of the biggest martial arts icons of the 1990s. The temperature was around 35 °C. I had just finished my Thai boxing training and was relaxing. My partner Leigh and I ate Pad Pak Boong Fai Daeng and rice, one of our favourite Thai dishes. Suddenly, her small black Samsung phone beeped. There was a message from a local talent agent. A movie was casting and they wanted her to attend. The audition was the following Monday. There was no description of what kind of film it was, or who the lead actor was. Seven days later, I travelled with her to the audition to provide her with moral support. We hopped into a cab and made our way through the congested streets. Forty minutes later, we arrived at a massive tower block. The casting office was on the 7th floor of the building. A gentleman introduced himself as Dear, he welcomed us into his office. He told us he was the casting director for the film. He was auditioning for a movie called *Full Love*. I was amazed when he told me it starred Jean-Claude Van Damme.

Leigh prepared herself and entered the casting room and I patiently waited outside. After thirty minutes, Leigh left the room smiling and pleased with her performance. We started to leave when Dear said, "Why don't you cast?" Embarrassed, I replied, "No mate, I'm not interested!" Leigh nudged me and said, "Come on, give it a go." I resisted and said, "No, but thanks anyway!" Trying to leave, I thought it would be a waste of time as they wouldn't pick me anyway as I was no actor. Then Dear said to my surprise, "Well, can I take a photo please?" Leigh then jumped in and said, "Yes, he will." So I went along with it and he clicked away. I had a couple of photos taken, gave Dear my number and we left. I didn't think about it anymore and just put the offer down to some crazy life experience. I returned to my routine of running my export business. A few days passed and my phone rang one afternoon and to my shock, it was Dear. He said several more roles were uncast, so he wanted me to return to the casting office and audition for the film. I was reluctant to go but was eventually swayed by Leigh and our friends after a beer. I asked some guys around the pool if they would like to come to the casting and they said they would love to. The last time I acted was in a play about *King Arthur* in my primary school years, which I hated. It was a pleasure to have some friends audition with me, so we could all look stupid together!

We piled into a cab and headed to the production house. When we entered the casting office, we had no idea what to expect or what we were doing. A lady greeted us. She gave us a form to fill out and said, "Write down your contact details." As she walked to another room, she said, "I will get your sides." I replied, "Ok!" We all looked at each other, wondering what the hell sides were. I didn't have a clue. The lady entered the casting room and quickly emerged with a few small A5 pieces of paper with the script printed on them. She passed them out to each one of us and asked us to read them in pairs. After a few minutes of reading, she asked us to run the lines and interact with each other as if we were in the scene. She said, "You have 10 minutes to practice. You are going to play sex tourists!" I smiled and looked at the others. Judging by their faces, everyone was trying to figure out how to pull it off.

Ten minutes later, we entered the rehearsal room. A Canon DSLR camera was in front of us, with the casting lady operating it. Dear played the role of a cab driver. Four plastic chairs were placed in the centre of the room as taxi seats. Dear was sitting in the front seat, pretending to be the taxi driver, holding a steering wheel. It seemed very childish to me. Grown men pretending to be in a taxi zooming around Bangkok.

The female casting director called "Action!" Then Dear said, "Where do you want to go?" We wannabe actors were lost for words. I quickly replied. "Sukhumvit Road mate!" Dear replied, "You want ladies, BOOM! BOOM! I can take you." I answered back, "Mate, we just want a beer!" We all looked at each other, not knowing what to say. Finally, the casting director said, "CUT! Casting over!" The audition was so quick and I didn't take it too seriously. Dear asked us could he take a few photos and videos separately of us. I talked about my life experiences and Dear recorded it and that was it. Then we were on our way home and had a few beers. I wasn't expecting a callback or anything. We made a complete balls up of the casting. Well, that's what I thought anyway. Three days later, my phone rang it was Dear. I picked up the phone and was expecting him to say that I hadn't gotten the movie role.

To my utter surprise he said, "Jean-Claude loved your casting tape Byron. Congratulations. The character you're playing isn't a sex tourist but a gangster. I will email you your start date and you will have to do a bit of fighting. I have arranged for you to be on set, so you can see how things are done. To begin with, we will take you to the shooting range, where you will train with the Royal Thai Police. Our minivan will pick you up at noon on Thursday." I thanked him, put the phone down and shouted, "FUCK YEAH!" I was looking forward to my upcoming adventure. My acting bug had just started and my first gig was with the iconic action movie hero and world-renowned martial artist hailing from Belgium, Mr. Jean-Claude Van Damme!

The day had come for me to go to the set and meet the filming team. While pouring my morning coffee, I suddenly heard a lot of commotion down the hallway. There was a crashing sound. I peeked outside into the hallway and saw a group of security guards breaking down a door just six doors down from mine. The apartment belonged to a Japanese guy named Mr. Yamato. Shouting and screaming came from his apartment. Initially, I thought it was an eviction, but unfortunately, it ended up being something much more sinister than that. The guards had truncheons and forced their way into Mr. Yamato's apartment. There was yelling in Japanese and Thai, then silence. Finally, one security guard spoke with me and assured me there was nothing to worry about. He said to me in Thai, "Mai Pen Rai." Translated into English, it means no problem! I was dubious about this, but the screaming and yelling died down and they seemed to have the problem under control. I watched the situation for a while to ensure everything was safe. I was worried about being late for my first day on a film set. I hung around for a short while, then I had to leave. I was running late and the van driver had just called to say he was waiting for me. After getting my bag and saying goodbye to Leigh, I proceeded to the lift. She watched me leave. I gestured to her to get back inside.

The minivan took thirty minutes to reach Somerset Suites, a high-class apartment building on Sathorn Road. I waited in the lobby, not knowing who was who. An assistant came to me and I was introduced to a very courteous young man called Kristopher Van Varenberg. Son of Jean-Claude Van Damme. Kris briefly discussed the day's events, then introduced me to the cast and crew. Martial arts icon Jean-Claude Van Damme appeared ten minutes later. Kristopher introduced me to his father. It was surreal to see the *Bloodsport* and *Kickboxer* star standing a few feet away from me in person. I had seen Jean-Claude in countless movies. The guy was a legend and influenced millions of people in a constructive way. Many thousands of people started kickboxing and weight training because of him. When I was younger and his films hit the screens, everybody wanted to be like Jean-Claude. The films *Kickboxer* and *Bloodsport* influenced me to go to Thailand. In fact, the first gym I trained at when I first went to Thailand was Sor Thanikul. This gym was where Jean-Claude asked to fight Tong Po in kickboxer. The gym was renamed Sor Kiet in the movie. Although I've been in many crazy circumstances, I never thought I would be in the company of the legend himself. I shook hands with Jean-Claude. He thanked us all for being there and told us what was expected of us. He talked to us for around ten minutes. It was like being in a new family. Finally, he told us to enjoy our day's training. We all got into two minivans and headed to the shooting range to train for the movie. What a start to the day! I was in a different world!

Thirty minutes later, we arrived at the Royal Thai Police shooting range on the outskirts of Bangkok. There were various weapons on display, including pistols, machine guns and pump-action shotguns. There were about twenty booths where you could shoot a variety of weapons. We got kitted out with safety goggles and ear protectors and headed to the shooting range. I was told we would be shooting pistols, as this was the primary weapon they would use in the film.

Actor Adam Karst and a Policeman were the instructors. Adam told me he had previously served in the Israeli army. His firearm knowledge impressed me. He demonstrated what was expected of us. His ability to shoot with the Beretta pistol was superb. Within seconds, he could load a magazine, shoot on target and load the clip again. During his first months in the Israeli army, he told me he spent three months loading the magazine into the gun and practicing shooting on target. You could tell. He told me the main firearms they used in the film would be semi-automatic Beretta nine-millimetre pistols. Firing a Beretta professionally is more complex than you think. I had shot guns before, so I thought it would be easy. But, oh no! I got picked up on many points. First, they ran through safety procedures and showed us how to handle the gun correctly. I learned some key points from Adam and the Thai instructor that day.

After the shooting range, we were taken to the film location, a massive car park on the outskirts of Bangkok. This is where they were shooting some of the film's action scenes. When I entered the movie set, I was taken aback. I was on a real movie set for the first time in my life, a once-in-a-lifetime opportunity. It was like a production line. Everyone worked in synch. The Thai film crew worked hard, setting up lights and monitors and cleaning the set for the next take. The stunt performers prepared for their scenes, running through their choreography. It was amazing. What an opportunity I was given and I lapped it up. I enjoyed watching the mechanics of how everything was working on the set. They were in the middle of one of the movie's action scenes, I stood to the side and watched patiently. The set consisted of a VW minibus, a taxi and a group of bad guys hanging around. The director called, "Quiet on set, get ready for the next take!" Jean-Claude came out of the wardrobe department, returned to the set and entered a taxi. The director said, "We are going for a take. Quiet on the set. Roll sound. Roll the camera. Action!" Jean-Claude then exited the taxi and confronted the villains, who were holding a lady they were trying to bundle into a minibus. Jean-Claude walked forward and one of the thugs threw a traffic control barrier at him. Then "CUT" was shouted by the assistant director. Crews ran around setting up the next take. Everyone involved was a true professional. I knew I wanted more of this. I was buzzing. This was just a taste of what was to come in my career.

Even though the scene was quickly shot, the attention to detail was incredible. From the lighting to the actors' performances, every element came together seamlessly in a flash. It's amazing how much was packed into such a short moment. If you watch the trailer for the film on YouTube, you will see this sequence. After being there for two hours, it was time to leave. Before leaving, I noticed a guy standing at the entrance to the parking area. He monitored everything that was going on. The guy looked angry and security refused to let him in. He started yelling abuse and the guards escorted him away. Later, I discovered he wanted to act in the film but wasn't accepted, he was upset. It was one of the first nutters I encountered in the movie business. I didn't realise it then, but there were many more to come. We left the film set and the van took me home.

I was tired but excited and on a high. Later that evening, I was relaxing at home. Leigh told me what caused the commotion in the hallway. She said, "A security guard was walking through the car park area 15 floors below. Suddenly, a Bonsai tree struck him on the head, knocking him to the ground and splitting his head open. Several other security guards helped their fellow guard to his feet and found a note attached to the Bonsai tree. It read, "We are being held hostage in room 1509. Please help us." I was dumbfounded after Leigh told me this, as he seemed like such a nice quiet guy. She said, "Despite Mr. Yamato's attempts to stop them from entering, security guards overwhelmed him. After the guards had forced their way in, they entered the bathroom to find two undernourished ladies held captive." They say you've got to be careful of the quiet ones and that rang so true with this guy. He would never look you in the eye if you passed him and looked like a harmless geek.

There was a small vent in the shower room which they had managed to prise open to throw down the tree. We learned after the incident that Mr. Yamato kept the poor lady's prisoners for over six months. For weeks, they tried in vain to get security's attention. They attached notes to shower bottles, toothbrushes and whatever they could find to chuck out, then hurled them out of the broken vent. They hoped security would spot them on the ground below. That day, the ladies must have gone for broke. Yamato left his beloved Bonsai tree in the bathroom after watering it. Yamato then left for the shop, locking the apartment door behind him. Not long after he was gone, one of the ladies launched the plant out of the window and it finally hit the mark like a cruise missile. Mr. Yamato returned from shopping, unaware of what had happened. Moments later, security arrived and the sordid episode was over.

The ladies finally got their freedom. They were angry at the security guards for not noticing all the notes they had thrown down. The crazy thing was that because the apartment block didn't want any bad publicity, they didn't call the police and solved the issue internally. The ladies Yamato held captive had to be compensated before Mr. Yamato could leave. He also had to compensate the apartment managers and ultimately, the injured security guard. The security guard had the biggest payday of his life, even though the apartment building took a 50 percent cut. After that incident, the apartment manager warned all residents not to throw things over the balcony. If they did, they would receive a 5,000-baht fine! Amazing!

A few days after this crazy incident, my first filming day arrived. I was looking forward to this day. I got myself shaved, cleaned up and looking fresh. I was picked up early, we convoyed to the north of Bangkok, arriving at a Chinese temple on the west bank of the Chao Phraya River. The temple was called Che Chin Temple. The temple had a beautiful pagoda and a courtyard with many fat Chinese Buddha's. It reminded me of one of those temples you see in the Chinese Kungfu movies. Next to the temple was a wooden house. The house was where the caretaker lived and this was our base camp. I looked inside, a lovely old lady was sitting in a rocking chair and must have been the caretaker.

The crews were running around her with lights and cables and setting up reflection boards and it seemed like it didn't bother her. She took it in her stride, sitting in her rocking chair and eating her peanuts! She probably didn't even know who Jean-Claude Van Damme was.

After a brief walk around, I was taken to the dressing area, where I was kitted out in my costume. The outfit consisted of black jeans, a black t-shirt and black shoes. After that, I was escorted to the makeup tent. My makeup artist powdered my face to make it less shiny and then I was done. I was given a script and briefed on what would happen in the scene by the assistant director. He said, "The scene we are shooting today involves you three bad guys getting out of a minivan and drawing batons looking for Frenchy. Jean-Claude Van Damme's character is Frenchy. You guys enter the house and a big fight starts. But we won't shoot that for a few days. We have many shots to complete before we get there." That was pretty straightforward and I was ready to go with whatever they said.

The props department gave me a black telescopic baton, my weapon for the scene. Initially, I thought I would be called immediately to work on set. How wrong was I? I waited eight hours to shoot. Any actor will tell you that if you want to work in the industry, you will spend hours waiting for your scene to be shot. I made the most of it and took in what was taking place around me as much as possible. I watched the actors on the monitors and I meticulously observed everything the gaffers and crew were doing. Jean-Claude directed this film and I was impressed by his attention to detail.

I got used in the afternoon. In my first scene, we drove around the Chinese temple entrance. The three of us got out of the van, looked around and drew our batons. The director called, "Cut, back to the first position." We returned to the van and repeated the whole process about half a dozen times. It was then I realized how important continuity was. I always remember Ron Smoorenburg telling me about when he fought Jackie Chan on the rooftop in Holland. It took over three to four weeks of twelve-hour days to shoot a ten-minute fight sequence because they needed the lighting the same every day. It's all about repeating the same action every time and everything must be correct. It can take one take or twenty takes until it's done right.

Finally, after some time, we must have got the shot and Jean-Claude shouted, "It's a wrap!" My twelve-hour working day ended! What an experience! After being guided off the set, I returned to the wardrobe, changed and sat outside, ready to be taken home. While waiting to go home, Jean-Claude approached me and said, "Well done today, you did a great job. Why did you cut your hair and shave? I prefer you to be unshaven and have unkempt hair. You look good on film. The camera loves you." I replied, "Really? I thought it was ok for me to have a shave and haircut before I went on set?" Jean-Claude said, "No, you look better unshaven, something to remember. Tonight, we are returning to the other side of the river by speed boat. Have a good evening. See you tomorrow."

It was a day to remember. We cruised down the Chao Phraya in speedboats, weaving in and out of river traffic and arrived at the Oriental Hotel. From there, a minibus took me home.

The following day was the same routine. The assistant director told me the lighting had to match the first shots we took the day before because of the sun's direction. We started filming our sequence of getting out of the Volkswagen and looking around for Frenchy to match the continuity. We slowly approached the house where the fight was going to happen. We exited the VW minibus, repeating the same sequence we had done countless times before. This time, a member of our team cautiously stepped inside the house. I waited outside the house's entrance, keeping a guard so Frenchy couldn't escape. I was the main focus of the camera. Despite my anxiety, I tried to remain calm. Jean-Claude did not appear in this scene and he watched the monitors directing the action.

Having the camera focused on you is a big deal for a movie first timer. You have so many thoughts running through your head. I thought in one of the takes, "This is taking a long time. Jesus, let's get it done!" I looked up at the sky and frowned, losing my concentration. It was hot that day, around 35 °C. I was getting tired. Jean-Claude then said through the microphone, "Byron!" It brought me back to my attention. I expected a bollocking. Instead, Jean-Claude said, "Well done, that's what I want!" I was surprised. What a fluke that was. He came over and said, "Byron, I want you to be as casual as possible in the next shot. Your character does this all the time. It's just another day for you. Relax! Pick your nose in the next take." I didn't know whether he was taking the piss or being serious. Regardless, I followed Jean-Claude's instructions. With my baton drawn, I gazed around and picked my nose when action was called. A sigh escaped my lips as I stared at the sky. Then, "Cut!" Jean-Claude congratulated me. I was chuffed. A wrap was called, we all took some photos together and I felt on top of the world. That was the end of my second shooting day!

The next few days were the same, a lot of waiting around and repeating the same sequence. Finally, we got closer to the house and went inside to shoot the internal shots. One day, I had the pleasure of witnessing my first ever stair fall. This was pure art in action. It's a dangerous stunt, as you could get severely injured doing it. I watched as the stunt guys helped each other put on back, arm, knee and chest protectors. Afterwards, they changed into the same clothes as the actors that they doubled. I stood patiently with the other actors, watching the action. The two stunt performers were at the top of the stairs. The second-unit director called action and the stunt guys nodded at each other as if to say, let's go! They tumbled down the stairs sideways. They really sold the shot. It looked great. They appeared to be knocked out when they hit the floor. "Cut!" Was called and they casually got up, brushing themselves off. They made it look so easy. These guys had worked on films such *as Bangkok Dangerous, The Expendables* and dozens more. The cool thing about this was, that they used the science of falling without injury. They spread the impact of the fall over a large portion of their back. They kept their chins tucked in and let gravity do the rest. The camera was angled at 45 degrees, so you couldn't see their faces. A thick crash mat was placed at the bottom of the stairs to stop them from rolling further. Afterwards, the two actors they were doubling would be brought in and told to lay where the stunt guys had fallen. This was yet another on-set experience that I thoroughly enjoyed. My days were getting better and better.

The following day, I waited to be called. I overheard some of the actors on set talking about the cinematographer and what a legend he was. Back then, I didn't know anything about cameramen or the technical side of things with movies. The actors commented on how proud they were to work alongside this chap. His name was Douglas Milsome. I had seen him behind the camera, he was friendly and English. I didn't realise it at the time he was the cinematographer for some excellent motion pictures like *The Shining, A Clockwork Orange and Full Metal Jacket*. After hearing that, I knew I was in highly regarded company and needed to make my finale scene as outstanding as possible. During the week's filming, some shots were filmed by another talented cinematographer, Ross Clarkson.

After spending just over a week on the set, my big day finally came. My crash course in working on my first film was ending. I was going out in style by receiving a carefully planned head kick from the legend, Mr. Van Damme. This was something to put in my history book of life experiences. That morning on set, I started to loosen up and stretch. I went to see some stunt guys who showed me how to react to the kick. I wanted to make it as good as possible. I didn't think my movie career was going any further than this movie, I was going to make the most of it. The stunt guys told me to loosen up my body. Once I received the kick, I needed to jerk my head back, fall backwards and then fall to the floor. I did many neck-stretching exercises because I did not want to get whiplash. The stunt guys ran through the technique with me for an hour and then I got it right. I was told to relax and wait for my call on set. I was due to shoot after lunch. I was taken to the set for a walk-through of what they needed to film and how my death scene would be filmed. The stunt coordinator showed me my movements. It was left to me to run through the sequence on my own. This gave me another opportunity to practice the sequence and get comfortable with the action. It allowed me to figure out how to make it look as realistic as possible before performing the stunt.

After 20 minutes, I was instructed to report to my first position. I got the nod and action was called. I carefully crept around the back of the house and up some stairs to find Frenchy. My brain spun with a million tiny anxieties, each one whispering questions about my performance. I pushed them aside and focused on the task, determined to do a good job. The assistant director said to me, "Walk slowly and cautiously so the camera can focus on you." I reverted to my original position. The assistant director said, "Ready for the take. Action!" The telescopic baton was in my hand. Mentally, I was planning to beat someone up with the baton this time. While watching and listening carefully, I walked around the balcony like a predator stalking its prey. Eventually, I came to a doorway that led to the top of the house, I paused. Then the assistant director said, "Cut, we've got it! Let's move on!"

I took a moment to relax and got a bottle of water. The first sequence was over. Now onto the second and final sequence. The crew moved the camera inside the house. This time, the camera would focus on both me and Frenchy. Twenty minutes later, the set was ready. I was asked to do a dummy run with Frenchy, so he could set up his kick. I waited a few steps from the balcony door. I slowly walked forward and Frenchy threw a gentle reverse kick at me, which landed just in front of my throat. He was happy, the timing was spot on. He nodded to me and said, "Let's go!" I took a few steps backwards. This was my big moment. I took a deep breath and stepped forward into the doorway. Frenchy was waiting for me, as I cautiously walked through the door. He threw a right reverse sidekick, which hit me in the throat. Bang on target! I reacted as best as I was capable of and fell to the floor, dead!

My character had been killed by the power of the kick, snapping my neck. I didn't move. Then, "Cut!" Was called. The stunt guys checked if I was OK. Jean-Claude quickly ran to the camera monitors to check the shot. He appeared very happy and the crew erupted in applause. We got it in one take. My grin stretched from ear to ear. One thing I want to say about the scene is that Jean-Claude's timing was spot-on. The kick was so quick and gentle that it was like someone had flicked you with their finger. To sell the kick even more, I reacted as best as I was able to by throwing my head backwards, making the kick look even more powerful. I fell to the floor and made my movement as big as possible. One unique thing was Jean-Claude's flawless control, precise timing and technique. I have been around many fighters and the kicking ability in Muay Thai is so powerful, which always impressed me. The tip-tap kicking in other arts never really did anything for me, as I was always taught about power kicks. That was until I met Jean-Claude Van Damme, the guy is a kicking master. His kicks are not only powerful, but they are also precise and have an almost balletic beauty to them. He combines the power and precision of his kicks with a sense of showmanship and grace that is truly captivating to watch. A true martial arts master! Many guys have tried to copy him in films, but none have hit the mark. The guy is unique and has an aura about him.

For the rest of the day, I was playing dead on the floor while they completed the interior shots. I lay there in between takes, observing what was going on out of the corner of my eye. It would be the first of many deaths in my acting career. The Muscles from Brussels inflicted my first movie death, something I am very proud of. After my day had ended, Jean-Claude thanked me and shook my hand. Kris told me I should take acting lessons and try theatre for experience. That night, I returned home happy with my performance. For the rest of the week, I was dead on the ground while they continued to fight inside the house. They needed me on the ground for continuity. Little did I know at the time that I would repeat this process many times in the future. Jean-Claude's ability to not only act and fight in the film but also direct and produce the project really impressed me. This is a mammoth task that takes a lot of commitment and balls. I admire him for doing it, there aren't many people who could. My filming time had ended at the temple and what a once-in-a-lifetime experience and opportunity that was. One thing I liked about Jean-Claude's family was that while they filmed in Bangkok, they adopted some Thai street dogs. They paid for their medical treatment and flew them back home with them. It was a very generous act of kindness and compassion.

Initially, I thought that was the end of my filming. Then I was told I would be needed again in a nightclub scene at a club called The White Rose. They filmed this in a massive mansion on the outskirts of Bangkok. It looked like a Hollywood mansion. It was an ideal location for the type of movie they were shooting. It was both grandiose and intimidating, with its lush grounds and imposing gates. It was also the perfect time to shoot, as darkness added to the ominous atmosphere. I was only needed in the background holding a pistol. In one scene, they had a party. I witnessed my first shoot-out scene one night.

This was extremely entertaining to watch. There was a bar scene where many of my fellow gangsters were hanging out and Frenchy walked in with his team. This can again be seen in the trailer for the film. I was amazed at how realistic the blood packs were. I stood by the stunt coordinator and the armourer and observed them putting squibs on the actors and stunt guys. Squibs are blood packs with a charge inside that can be remotely activated. The actor needs to react as soon as the squib explodes. This was fun to watch. In one scene, there was a whole group of gangsters sitting on the sofa near the bar area of the club. Many of the bad guys were shot by Frenchy and his associates. There was fake blood spluttering everywhere. I asked the stunt coordinator how they made the blood and he told me they boiled red corn syrup and mixed it with coffee. Then they would put it on a board and watch it drip down to see if it had the correct density of real blood. Once they got it right, they poured it into the plastic squib packs, ready for action. This is a technique for cooking blood that I use to this day.

I had another week of shooting at the White Rose. It was a complete filming education for me, watching all the action take place. When my time came to an end, I was happy. I thought some people would pay for this kind of experience. Little did I know at the time that many people already do that in the business. We were invited to the wrap party a few days later in one of Bangkok's big clubs. We enjoyed the food and drinks that were laid out for us. Our paths crossed at the bar with Jean-Claude's father, Mr. Eugene Varenbergh. He was a very friendly man. Leigh discussed her dance training with him. She demonstrated that she could kick well at one point. To cut a long story short, she threw a high kick straight up and nearly kicked Eugene in the head. It was a good thing that her control was exceptionally good, as she only missed him by only a few inches. Which was lucky for us, all of us laughed about it. It was the last time I saw Jean-Claude and many of the cast and crew and that was the end of my first ever movie. It was time to move on.

TAKE 2

After the Van Damme film, I returned to England for a few months to see family and friends. The local paper heard about my filming adventure. They used to do regular features on my Thai boxing school back in the day. They wrote a massive two-page centre spread about me, titled "How I got killed by the muscles from Brussels." It was good to get some publicity. After the break in England, we returned to Thailand and moved apartments. It was the end of an era of staying in the apartment block, many of our friends were leaving, plus the energy in the building didn't seem right anymore. The place started to have an unfriendly vibe. First, one of the residents sadly decided to base jump off the top of the building and he landed on top of the internet shop roof, instantly killing himself. A few days later, one of our friends spotted a poor Japanese guy dead in the pool. The unfortunate individual had succumbed to the water, yet the vigilant pool attendant was oblivious, as he was preoccupied with grooming himself behind the bar. Upon being notified by security, the pool attendant was still clutching onto his tweezers and mirror. He didn't have a clue! I kid you not!
After these experiences, we decided to get a new apartment in another area of town. Sukhumvit Soi 6 became our new

stomping ground. The film business wasn't exactly my life's calling, but I thought, why not see where it could go? For me, it was all about the adventure. I spread the word that I was game for any gig to soak up some experience. With yellow pages in hand, I got the contact details of a bunch of casting directors. With no fancy headshots, no showreel and a resume with one credit, my chances were slim, but we all need to start somewhere. I whipped up a DIY video of me with a toy gun, strutting my stuff like Rambo. Leigh snapped a cool picture and that was my audition package, which I sent to all these casting directors. A bit unorthodox, maybe, but hey, you've got to do what works.

A few weeks passed and I managed to land one short movie, which led me to get a role in a pretty good film. I didn't know it at the time, but the casting director of the short movie was auditioning for an upcoming Hollywood film. The character was cool a mercenary. They were filming in Kanchanaburi and on the river Kwai. This film featured the MMA fighter Fedor Emelianenko, Rutger Hauer and Michael Madsen. I was ready to go. Two weeks of craziness in Thailand's jungles, running around with machine guns and dodging explosions. Then, unfortunately, I couldn't do the movie because I got sick with Dengue fever. I was disappointed. Then things started to go from bad to worse. It started to kick off one night. March 26th, the rumour on the street was that the military was coming into the city to take over. There was an eerie silence in Bangkok. I wondered what was happening. I quickly turned on the TV and no stations were broadcasting. Then a military commander appeared on the screen and said the army was taking over the government. I had already experienced a coup in 2006, so I hoped this situation wouldn't develop into another one. Unfortunately, it did. Bangkok again was on lockdown. A series of political demonstrations followed, during the climax. The protests ended on April 14th, 2009. The shit hit the fan. It decimated the film industry for months. All films and TV commercials were cancelled. I honestly thought that the game was over for my little jaunt of acting and that would be that. How wrong was I?

Some of the local actors and stunt guys heard down the grapevine that there was a backlog of films due to shoot in Thailand because of the coup. I got my arse into gear and restarted my mission, as this would be a great way to get my credits up. To get my foot in the door of the local film industry, I popped down to the local photography studio. I paid around 2,000 baht (approximately 50 pounds) to have some professional headshots done. Then I scoured the internet for talent agencies, talent directors and film companies, contacting them all and sending my picture and contact details. As I learned the ropes of the film industry, I soon realised that you needed to be as diverse as possible. I needed to contact every kind of production to be a full-time actor, not only Western films but also Indian, Chinese and Korean. Another thing I learned was that I needed to be on all the agent's books to survive in the industry. Casting directors only work with specific agents or bookers in Bangkok. You have one casting director working for a company that only deals with Indian productions and another casting director will only focus on Hollywood productions etc. I spent hours sending my profile and skill set to every possible talent agent covering the whole field. It paid off and in no time, I was getting calls. Next, I contacted the stunt coordinators. I needed as much experience as possible to make a good new show reel. I was open to anything, to be honest with you. Finally, I landed a role in an independent short film called *The Art of Living*. This tells the story of a Western drug mule in Thailand employed by a London gangster. My character was a bodyguard in this film and I met some key individuals in the film industry. I managed to get confirmed on a few TV commercials. At the same time, I was being as proactive as possible. I had an idea to write a script called *Bareknuckle*.

Bareknuckle tells a story about what happened to me and some friends in the early 1990s. It's a crazy story, to be honest with you and it shows you how stupid you can be when you are young. Back then, we trained all over Thailand in Muay Thaia nd we got friendly with a boxing gym owner called Pyatt. He fought against phenomenal French Thai boxer turned actor Joe Prestia and even against England's pioneer of Muay Thai Ronnie Green in Paris in the 1980s. After a few months of training at his gym, Pyatt told us about an illegal tournament taking place in a stone quarry. This was on an island in southern Myanmar. There was a huge risk if we went. The country was a no-go zone. If we got caught by the authorities, we would have been put in prison. There were no rules and the only way fighters could win would be by knockout. Despite the risks, we felt like it was the opportunity of a lifetime and wanted to take it. Myanmar vs. Thailand, I thought, yeah, let us have some of that! The event lasted five days to celebrate the Chinese New Year. We were smuggled to the island with Southern Thailand's finest bare-knuckle boxers. A corrupt military commander from the island organised the event. Unfortunately for us, things became very dangerous and we had to escape the island.

Many people told me that this would be an excellent idea for a screenplay. I didn't know how to write a screenplay or present a film idea to producers back then. I researched how to present a film to potential investors, wrote a synopsis and made a poster. When I was invited to the Thai film festival, I printed some off and left them on some tables. As a result, the line producer from *Full Love* picked one up and called me a few weeks later. He was looking for a movie to produce. He wanted two synopses. I presented him with two film ideas, *Bareknuckle* and *The Art of Living*. The director of *The Art of Living* had artistic differences and the producer chose *Bareknuckle*. I thought this would be an excellent project to write with him, on the side while I cast for film roles. We agreed to meet twice a week to write the script. At the time, I was told about a producer who could place me in many American movies. I could basically buy parts in movies over a three-year period if I paid him $200,000, launching my acting career. I was unaware that actors could often purchase roles in films. As I did not have $200,000 to spare, I declined the offer and had to do it the hard way.

I studied basic acting and being yourself in front of the camera. I did this by using my camera and recording myself. I also tried to gather as much information as possible about how directors shoot some scenes in films and film terminology.

With the action side of things, I began to train in the first part of my journey by learning hit reactions in every way possible in a realistic manner. You must have seen some old films where an actor or stunt guy was hit or shot. I watched a lot of those scenes and studied how they were performed. I applied the same techniques to my own acting. I also practiced doing hit reactions in front of a mirror and experimented with different ways of performing them. This helped me fine-tune my techniques and develop my own style. I read about people getting shot in real life and studied videos. I researched many action films and copied their movements. When I first began training for hit reactions, I trained with friends at the gym. After a while, I started practicing with professional stunt guys, I had met on my first film and built my skill set up bit by bit, learning new skills from them. I trained to be hit in all areas of my body. The stunt guys taught me that you need to sell the shot for the camera and make the movements more prominent. Things looked very promising, I was confirmed on a few projects and many films were coming to Thailand.

Determined, I wanted to see how things unfolded after spending hours researching the film business and the options available. Reading about certain actor's careers inspired me. I craved to be like some of the old-school villains you would see in Clint Eastwood, Charles Bronson and Sergio Leone movies. They used the same guys repeatedly, but as different characters. It became clear to me that the key to success in any field was consistency and having a reliable set of skills and traits that could be applied to any role. It was also clear that having a strong work ethic and a willingness to learn were essential for any actor wanting to make a lasting impression in the film industry. I was always intrigued by the British wrestler Pat Roach. He worked on all the *Indiana Jones* movies and played the German Luftwaffe mechanic, who fistfights with Jones before being killed by the aircraft's propeller blades on the airstrip in Egypt. This guy had a steady stream of work and was an extraordinary fellow.

At one point, I thought about solely going down the stuntman route. I knew many stunt guys were getting film work and it was very lucrative. I spoke to some of the action guys in the industry. They told me that if I wanted to gain more acting roles in Asia, it was paramount that I could perform some stunts. However, I knew I did not want to jump off buildings, do car hits, or stunt double. I was getting too old for that. I appreciated that I didn't have the abilities of some of these amazing people. I asked a few people in the industry about both routes to take. One casting director told me, "99 percent of stunt guys cannot act. Casting directors won't take you seriously if they think you're a stunt guy. You can't do both. If you do too many movies as a stunt performer, many casting directors will class you as a stuntman and you won't get any acting roles." I didn't really understand that snobby logic. After playing around with the idea of being a stuntman, I decided to go down the acting route. However, I implemented a plan to learn some stunts that would suit my character, so stunt coordinators could also employ me.

I have worked on some movies and have been credited as a stunt performer. The jobs I got credited as a stuntman were playing the bad guy who gets shot, beaten, stabbed, killed, or blown up, but under one condition, I was always seen. I learned from guys in the industry that sometimes productions need someone to do some action and speak one or two lines. I planned that if I specialised in being shot, stabbed, or tortured, with my rugged look, I would get a constant work stream. I would also be one step ahead of the actors who didn't have that ability. I gathered that if you have a bad guy who looks mean on screen, he will make the main star seem so much more powerful. That's what the industry is about, selling the hero! I wasn't interested in playing the protagonist whatsoever, it was far too boring. Look at the crazy things that the bad guys get up to in films, causing mayhem that's right up my street. To top it off, you get paid for it, you are immortalised in film history and you don't get arrested!

Within two years, I planned to start landing one-liner speaking roles. Within five years, I wanted jobs outside Thailand. Within ten years, I wanted to play a film's main antagonist or antihero. I was confident in my abilities and felt that with the right opportunities and hard work, I could achieve my dream. I had a plan in place and was determined to stick to it. I was ready to put in the effort needed to achieve my goal. It was like a mountain climber looking up at a challenging peak and seeing the path ahead and all the steps needed to make it to the summit, but aware of the effort and dedication it would take to get there. I was ready to take on the challenge and if I fell off the mountain, at least I'd have a good story to tell, maybe I could write a book about it!

Things were going smoothly. Several TV commercials and film pilots were booked for me. Every month, I was offered new jobs. I received a call from a casting director. A film was coming to Thailand called *Largo Winch 2*, aka *The Burma Conspiracy*. They were casting for mercenaries. I brushed up on my firearm skills and collaborated with an action actor Ron Smoorenburg. Leigh was also casting for a part in the film and I helped her rehearse. Leigh and I went to the casting together and we met Ron there. Ron helped me my casting and vice versa. I assisted Leigh with her audition, which went smoothly. After we finished the casting, the casting director asked me if I could help someone else. I politely agreed, trying to be helpful. A guy appeared. I will call him The Texan.

He didn't stop talking about himself. I had seen him before on the set of the Van Damme movie, he was an extra. He got a bollocking for taking too many photos and had his camera taken away. He boasted of being Jean-Claude Van Damme's bodyguard for some unknown reason, but never was. It appeared that he had a chemical romance going on. His body was ripped, but in a synthetic way. He was stuck in the 1980s with his dress sense, a cross between Yul Brynner and Ming the Merciless, the main antagonist of the *Flash Gordon* franchise. Black jeans, a black t-shirt and a heavy silver necklace adorned this bald man. He proudly displayed a heavily dyed black horseshoe moustache. If the village people were auditioning, he would have gotten the role. He was just right for any cowboy or steam punk movie. Anyway, I got roped into helping the Texan with his audition. I asked him if he had anything choreographed. He replied, "Byron, I've had 47 registered street fights, all of which I've won by knockout.

I don't need to choreograph anything!" Alarm bells started ringing, what the hell was this geezer talking about? Doesn't he realise we are acting and it's not real? I did think at one point that he was method acting. If he was, he was rather proficient at it. I told him straight, "This is an audition. I need to know what you'll throw at me so I can react to it to make you look good." I said that so he fully understood that I was trying to help him out, as it's a two-way street, in fight auditions, you are supposed to help each other. The Texan stood back and proclaimed like a Greek god, "Byron! I look good! I've got this, you don't need to react. This role is mine."

I thought, OK, I will go and assist him with his casting to please the casting director. However, I proceeded with caution, as it seemed to me, he didn't understand what a casting like this involved. The casting director asked us to stay in the waiting room and when we heard action to enter the main room in character and perform our scene. The Texan's confidence was like a skyscraper, reaching high into the sky. He seemed to think he had it all figured out, but it was clear that he hadn't taken the time to truly understand the situation and the complexities involved. I waited patiently in the waiting room with him. This was intriguing. He was very jittery. I looked at his hands, they were shaking. Maybe this geezer was nervous or maybe he wasn't the full ticket. The room was filled with tension, like a bow string pulled back and waiting to be released.

The casting director called "ACTION!" The Texan stormed into the casting room with his emotions going through the roof. He shouted as if he were in some superhero movie, a bit like Thor. It would have gone down well in a theatre! I followed the Texan into the room and he turned and faced me. He was like a bull in a China shop! The Texan started throwing erratic punches as if he were doing the doggy paddle. He was like a man possessed. His eyes bulged as if he had just taken Viagra. He had a froth on his lips like a rabid fox. He nearly burst a blood vessel. My guard went up as soon as I saw those crazy, uncontrolled punches coming at me. I kept a tight high guard, the haymakers landed on my forearms. The chaotic and frenzied energy of the man was like a flood unleashed from a broken dam, uncontrollably surging forth with wild intensity. I wasn't going to get hit by those punches. Unsatisfied that his punches were not getting through my guard and I wasn't reacting, he threw a roundhouse kick at me, which I blocked. He paused in his madness. I put my guard down, thinking the flurry of punches was over, immediately he launched a right-handed punch at me, landing straight on my forehead. I stood there with my arms open as if to say, "What the fuck?" Then silence. His eyes were nervous. I don't know whether he threw the punch on purpose or couldn't control his anger. He was out of breath, puffing away with rage. The casting director nervously called, "CUT!" She asked if I was OK. I replied, "Yes, no problem."

Upon leaving the casting office, the Texan was calmer. He thought he had done a good job. He apologised to me and was friendly. Maybe he felt insecure, or maybe his nerves got the better of him during the audition. Perhaps the testosterone kicked in too much. It was like a switch had been flipped, as if his anger was a fleeting storm that cleared up just as quickly as it had arrived. I gave him the benefit of the doubt. He was having a hard time with money and asked if we could recommend him to any productions when they needed people. We told him that we would let him know about any productions and he should do the same. We shared a taxi to the centre of town. The Texan got out of the cab in downtown Bangkok. The cheeky bugger never gave us money for the cab.

A week later, I was confirmed on the project. A brand-new adventure was about to begin. Unfortunately for the Texan, he didn't get a part. Interestingly, the stunt coordinator from the film said to me, "After seeing The Texans audition and learning about his persona, I do not want The Texan anywhere near the movie. He's a liability to himself and everyone else." I met the director of the film, Jerome Salle, a few weeks after the casting. He was the first French director I ever worked with. Jerome had many great credits behind him and this was a great step in the right direction. He congratulated me on landing the role. He asked me to grow a beard. At the time, I was beardless. I remember Van Damme telling me to keep my stubble, as he said it suited me. Maybe they were right. Jerome told me I had three months to grow a full beard. The movie would star Sharon Stone, Tom Sisley and Clemens Schick. I would shoot in Bangkok, on the Thai-Burmese border and in Belgium. My role was that of a mercenary pilot. It would involve flying around in a Huey helicopter, shooting automatic weapons, fighting and a lot more.

This was right up my street. I had just secured my second international movie and I was going to be shooting in Belgium. Within two years, I had accomplished my goal of filming in a different country. I got into some serious training for the film. I upped my fitness regime. I started training in how to use automatic weapons properly and trained in screen fighting. I trained in hit reactions as we had a fight on a private jet. Life was great. Everything was on track. Prior to *The Burma Conspiracy,* I was booked on two Indian productions. However, as *Forest Gump* once said, "Life is like a box of chocolates. You never know what you're going to get!" It was certainly the case on the next job!

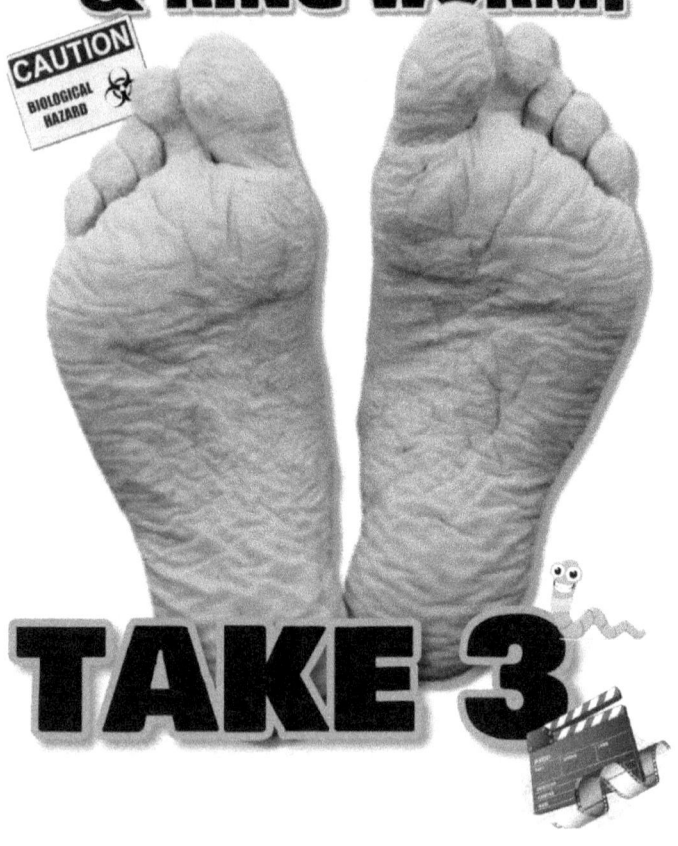

TAKE 3

One day I received a telephone call from a female talent agent, whom I will call Lady Marmalade. She only dealt with Indian movies and had a deal with a local production house. She told me there was a Southern Indian action movie filming and they needed a whole group of guys to play gangsters. It involved fighting and acting. I thought, why not add some Indian spice to my filmmaking career while I wait for the other film to start? It would be good to get my foot in the door of the Indian market. Every year, hundreds of Indian movies are shot in Thailand. In fact, some stunt teams receive enough work from Indian movies to keep them employed all year-round. The southern Indian film industry is called Telugu cinema and it's worth millions. In 2021, Telugu cinema was the largest film industry in India. Telugu films sold 233 million tickets in 2022. Hyderabad is the Telugu film industry's capital. It's only approximately 6 hours from Hyderabad to Bangkok and with cheap crews, Thailand is a no-brainer for these productions to film there. The casting for this film was in the Ladprao area of Bangkok. The cool thing was that the production had quite a few movies on their books. The casting location was in an industrial unit that was the stunt team's home.

When I entered the casting studio, five Indian guys sat at a table with the stunt coordinator. There were many actors and stuntmen casting. I watched the auditions. It was like a buffet, with everyone bringing their own talents and skills to the table for consideration. Some of the guys I had never seen before on the action circuit. The stuntmen and actors began casting one by one. Several of the guys there had exceptional talents. Some guys did backflips, some impressive spinning kicks and some impressive acrobatics. When it was my turn, I felt out of depth to be honest with you. I stuck to what I knew. I couldn't do backflips or these high spinning jumping kicks, so I did some Thai shadowboxing and showed them some hit reactions, which I knew I was proficient at. After my casting, they confirmed me and booked me for the film. It is important to remember that every movie should have characters of all ages and different looks. Most thugs would have different fighting abilities and qualities if they were in a gang. There would be the overweight and small guys, one could be a great kicker and the other could be a great wrestler. I got my foot in the door of another production and film market, leading to more future films. I was on the film shoot one week later. The location was close to where we filmed the Van Damme movie.

Located near Chinatown, the film location was an old, bonded warehouse. It was used in Hollywood films such as *The Hangover* Part 2, *American Gangster*, *The Deer Hunter* and *Ong Bak*. Due to its isolation, line producers often used this location. The warehouse was also easy to access and provided plenty of space for filming. Furthermore, it was far from residential zones and the sound of filming was unlikely to disturb anyone. The mighty Chao Phraya River was behind the warehouse. For more than 225 miles, the river flows through the fertile central plains to the Gulf of Thailand. Nine hundred and forty-eight canals flow into that river. Over 387,000 tonnes of garbage have been pulled out of it since 2015. However, that waterway is truly unique. Due to the high levels of pollutants, the river has become a breeding ground for an array of species of parasites and diseases that can be transferred to humans. In addition, the channel is home to a multitude of fish species, some of which have mutated due to the chemical runoff. The situation is like Pandora's Box, where you never know what will come out next. The water appears serene and tranquil, but beneath the surface lies a hidden danger waiting to be unleashed.

My fellow bad guys and I arrived early on set at 7 a.m. We ate breakfast provided in white polystyrene take-out containers. Breakfast was Pat Gai Kai Dow, which translates to English as fried rice with chicken and an egg placed on top. There was a group meeting after breakfast with the second unit director. He explained what the film was about. An Indian engineering student in the U.S. gets in trouble with local gangsters and must resolve his problems to return to his lady love in India. If you didn't know, the second unit director, or action director, oversees all film action sequences. For example, a movie with numerous fights or car crashes always has a second-unit action director. You may have seen many films heavy on action and not realised that there are two directors. Many standard film directors don't know action choreography, so they employ a stunt coordinator or fight choreographer who choreographs the action or fight scenes in the film. They will pre-shoot each action scene with their team, which the principal director approves. This helps to save time and money during shooting, as the director will have the fight or action scene pre-planned and pre-shot. This also ensures that the actors are safe when shooting the action sequences, as the stunt coordinator will have put safety protocols in place.

The second unit director told us that the filming would begin in a bar inside the warehouse during the movie's first sequence. This was to establish us as the bad guys. He explained that our main boss was a people trafficker from Columbia called Charlie. He had young girls held captive in some trucks within the building. Charlie would sit on a sofa in a bar area of the building and make a deal with the lead character, Viswa. Suddenly, the lights would go out and a fire would start. Once the lights return, Viswa flips a table, which crashes into some of our fellow villains and they fall to the ground.

Next, the rest of us gangsters attack and fight Viswa. Who single-handedly takes on all ten of us, knocking us to the ground with a flurry of kicks and punches just like *Superman.* Two of our henchmen aim guns at Viswas's head during the chaos. He swiftly disarms them, snatching the two guns out of their hands. Finally, he backs up and aims the two pistols at us all, John Wick style, to stop us from advancing. A tense standoff establishes on all the bad guys' faces. He finally releases the magazines from the pistols, which drop to the ground slowly. Cut! That was the end of the first sequence.

It seemed intense, but I loved it. The task ahead was comparable to putting together a puzzle, piecing together all the details from the different elements of the scene in sequence to craft a cohesive final product. Filming would start 3 hours later. While I had some time on my hands, I investigated the warehouse and surroundings we were shooting in. I ventured inside the warehouse and there were 20 vehicles parked in all kinds of positions. All the cars were American because, although they were filming in Thailand, they were cheating the shots for America. There was many classic vintage American cars and some army trucks. I presumed the army trucks would be incarcerating some of the female prisoners. In a corner of the warehouse a team of guys were drilling holes into lots of 4-inch blue piping. They were making a massive rig that was around 20 feet long. I asked one of the guys assembling the piping what they were making and he said, "We are making a water rig." I watched as they put this massive square rig together and attached it to a hose trailing outside the building. Then they winched the rig up to the ceiling. It was like a garden sprinkler system, but in the air. Over at the bar area, an elderly guy and his team made a bar from pallets and old boxes. One of his guys pasted old newspapers on the wall. Two guys placed a sofa and a small, lightweight coffee table in the bar area. Next, a guy from the special effects department dressed the scene with sugar glass bottles. Sugar glass bottles are made from syrup, water and sugar. To prevent actors from being injured, these bottles are used in action scenes instead of glass. Although it is not as dangerous as real glass, it still has the potential for injury from shards. After a short time, the set was prepped and ready for action.

I walked through the massive warehouse and gazed at the mighty Chao Phraya River. Giant green Evergreen container ships cruised by, meandering through the stream. To the right of me, I spotted an antique fire truck from the 1950's. It was just like the one from the Keystone Cop TV series. It intrigued me, as I thought it should be in a museum. It even had a brass bell instead of a siren. The driver was a few metres away and chucked a yellow hose into the waterway. He started the engine on the back of the fire truck and pumped water from the river into the truck. I was planning to sit and chill, watching the tankers pass by. However, it was very noisy because of the water pump on the fire engine. I decided to leave and get lunch.

After lunch, we were summoned to the warehouse and told our positions were set. During the dummy run, Viswa and Charlie rehearsed the dialogue and movements for the scene, to make sure everyone was familiar and comfortable with the blocking and delivery of the lines. This way, when it was time to shoot the scene, everything would go as smoothly as possible. We quickly got into position and the director shouted, "Action!" We ran through the scene. All of us bad guys stood still, looking mean. After the actors finished their dialogue, the lights were turned off and "Cut!" Was called. This was our cue to prepare for the action sequence. Crews checked the film set and ensured that the continuity of the scene was correct. In the next step, the stunt coordinator gathered the villains together and ran through the choreography with each of us individually. As a team, we had to work together in unison. Hence, if one of the guys didn't do the choreography correctly, the whole scene wouldn't work. When one of our guys was fighting Viswa, the guys in the background had to act as if they were ready to attack. After the stunt coordinator was satisfied, we returned to our first positions and prepared for action. We started the scene in the dark and waited.

As the lights went on, Viswa flipped up the table, hitting two of our bad guys. As one of our fellow villains tried to attack him, he front-kicked him over. When the guy fell to the ground, I was to the right of the shot and my job, was to come forward with the other team members so that the camera could focus on our faces individually, establishing our identities. This scene was designed to establish the characters as a formidable villainous team and create suspense. The Mexican standoff was used to build tension and create dramatic moments for the audience. We shot the scene in about 3–4 takes before moving on to the next section.

We did a dummy run with the choreographer and went through the fight scene. It started like this, two of our guys would draw guns and point them at Viswa. They would both be disarmed by him with some quick Aikido moves. One of the guys gets hit in the head with an elbow from Viswa and stumbles back in a daze. Viswa then turns the guns onto us bad guys and the camera focuses again on all our faces. Viswa releases the magazines from his guns and he challenges us and we all run at him. One by one, he knocks us down with a flurry of kicks and punches. One guy gets a bottle smashed on his head and another gets thrown onto one of the cars. In all the chaos, another bad guy gets his face smashed through a television. Viswa escapes and runs to the back of the warehouse. Then, "Cut!" Was called. We all returned to our first starting position. It reminded me of growing up in England in the late 1980s and what happened in some pubs I frequented. I wish I had Viswa with me then. The same thing happened in those pubs, except it was beer bottles, not car windows. And the TV was usually broken by the end of the night!

After lunch, we moved onto the end sequence of my fight scene. We would meet Viswa at the back of the warehouse. This time, a fire would break out in the background and the sprinkler system would be activated. In the rain, we would fight. We attack him again, but this time it's more intense. I would charge at Viswa and throw two haymaker punches at him. I would react in pain when Viswa blocked my two strikes. Finally, Viswa would punch me eight times in the stomach, which I would need to react to. He would push my head to the side, knocking me to the ground. I would be knocked out! Job done! I was raring to get started, as it was going to be lying on the ground for a week doing nothing and getting paid for it!

Now, moving onto my final scene in the movie. The props department lit a fire a few feet from the bar. They turned on a large bunch of fans and simultaneously, the sprinkler system started working. It looked impressive. The director over the speaker shouted, "Ready, ready! Action!" We ran under the sprinkler system, which was very noisy with the water and the fans blowing. Then, one by one, we attacked Viswa like a pack of wolves! Visually, it looked amazing. My fellow villains fought Viswa and were quickly knocked out. Then it was my turn. I marched forward and attacked Viswa. I could hardly see anything because of the intensity of the rain. In spite of this, I threw two haymaker punches at him and he quickly parried them. Next, Viswa rabbit punched my stomach and threw me like a rag doll to the floor. There were no mats and I fell hard on the concrete, doing an Ukemi fall from Judo. I splashed into the dirty water. Easy money, I thought! Job done! I was in for a surprise when I found out that I would have to repeat the same fall multiple times. Doing Ukemi falls on the concrete floor without mats can be dangerous and after a few times, the bruises started to show. Even though it was hard work, I was glad to have completed the whole fight scene.

I was so tired when we changed out of our wet costumes. Lady Marmalade hadn't brought towels for us. So, we had to stand around to get dry. The Indian star playing Viswa had a dressing gown given to him and assistants taking care of him, drying him down and treating him like a king. He also had a comfortable, cosy trailer with a shower. We had nothing. After a long, wet shooting day, we headed home like drowned rats. It was a class divide, where one person was treated like royalty and the others were left with no resources to get dry and return home in a dignified manner.

During the rest of the week, while they completed the fight scene, my fellow bad guys and I played dead. We were to stay on the ground while soaking in the water. The days dragged on and we were sprayed every ten minutes, on and off, until "Cut!" Was called. It was extreme Japanese water torture. It was excessive, we had to spit out the water as it dribbled into our mouths. There was no way of escaping it. Now lying on the ground for 30 minutes or an hour is not so bad. However, when you are lying on concrete for 8 hours a day, being sprayed with muddy, fishy water gets a bit much. You could taste the sediment in the water. Some guys got pissed off with it so they covered their heads with their jackets not caring about continuity. I remember looking at a guy called Anton, who was an outstanding stuntman and director and we laughed at each other. It was such a ridiculous situation and complete madness. During the takes, I crawled outside, where the water fell. Eventually, I was on the edge of it but still lying in a massive, dirty puddle. At this point, I thought, Fuck the continuity, but I had to stay to get paid. Lady Marmalade eventually used her brain and brought us towels in the end. However, she never dried our clothes, so every day we had to put on wet clothes, which was horrible. This lady's logic baffled me. I had to powder my feet every night to dry them out. The condition of my feet was so bad that they looked like rotten flesh. I was concerned that I would get trench foot.

We were thrilled when the shoot was over. Lady Marmalade binned our clothes. She paid us and left without a care in the world, counting her bundles of cash. When we left the location, we looked out of the back of the van. The Keystone Cop firetruck driver disconnected a hose that trailed inside the building to the rain rig. We all returned home silently when we realised the water was from the river. We couldn't believe it, cheeky bastards! Trust me, it was an experience. But unfortunately, the worst was yet to come.

It took a few days for my feet to recover from the film job. After being sprayed with dirty water, my skin resembled a wrinkled pink bag. A red mark appeared on my neck. I didn't overthink it initially, but it wouldn't go away after four or five days. I became extremely paranoid. Every once in a while, I checked the mirror to see if it was going away, but it never did. My skin became itchy and I had patches of white-looking fungus appearing. Fungi grew between my toes and to top it off, I had a nasty bout of the flu! As the days went on, I felt myself sinking deeper and deeper into a quagmire of sickness and despair. I Googled the river and it came up with this. "Recent Greenpeace reports found high levels of toxic pollution in the Chao Phraya. A study found heavy metals, hormone-disrupting chemicals, human carcinogens and dangerous sediments." I googled human carcinogens and discovered it was a substance capable of causing cancer. I decided to see a local doctor to get peace of mind.

The doctor asked me what was wrong. I showed him the red marks on my neck, arms and feet. He carefully examined the red patch and cauliflower fungus using a magnifying glass. Then, looking at the nurse assisting him, he spoke in Thai. "Bah Bah Ba Boor Felang!" Translated into English, it means crazy foreigner. I knew something wasn't right. Then he asked me, "Have I been swimming in sewage?" I replied, "It's not something I would do. I was on a movie set and they sprayed us with river water. Why?" The doctor was dumbfounded. He said, "You're crazy! Do you realise that 40% of liquid waste is discharged directly into the channel untreated? Fewer than 2 percent of households in the city have access to sewage systems, you could have contracted cholera and more! You have a fungus and bacteria called Schistosomiasis, known as Bilharzia. The infection is caused by a parasitic worm that lives in fresh water in subtropical regions. There is also a possibility that you will need to be treated for Weal's disease." It was getting worse! The doctor wrote me a prescription and an invoice. The invoice was for 5,000 Baht, which is approximately 113 pounds. The doctor looked at me and smiled, shaking his head. He told me, "Do not to share towels!"

When I arrived home, I was like a man possessed. I covered myself with creams and antibiotics. It took two weeks for the fungus and red marks to disappear! Finally, the blood tests came back and I was still human. The budget for this film was a staggering 3.8 million U.S. dollars. They did have the money to do things right. Perhaps the Indian production was unaware of where the water came from. Still, the line producing company that arranged the locations surely knew, as did Miss Marmalade. When circumstances like these arise, it is usually due to greedy productions trying to cut corners and save money. Working in Asia sometimes means taking risks. There are no unions to support you. I should have walked off, but I wanted the cash and the credit. It was hard-core film making!

Several years after my Indian action movie experience, a friend of mine, Dave Blazejko, was fighting in a film in the same area. During the fight, the film's main star kicked him and he fell backwards. He thought that if he fell into the river, it would enhance the dramatic effect of the scene. It did and the director loved it. Dave regretted it later. In a similar way to mine, he contracted a severe ear infection and a skin infection. Following the shoot, he was in pain down the left side of his face and went to the hospital. Syringes were inserted into his ears and tests were conducted. His left ear was filled with a pussy-green liquid. After analysing it, the doctor was amazed. Crazy Dave learned his lesson like me and ended up 5,000 Baht worse off after the doctor examined his ear and told him it was infected with syphilis. If you plan to film near that river, I suggest you avoid it like the plague!

Many of the guys in that Indian film turned out to do remarkable things. Some ventured into directing and some filmed with The Rock, Keanu Reeves and Jackie Chan. This job led me to a recommendation to work with the *Face Off, Mission Impossible* director, the legendary John Woo. All these opportunities were made possible by the humble beginnings of doing crap jobs. It was through these experiences that I was able to build up my contacts, gain recognition and eventually be in a position to work with Hollywood directors. Unfortunately, I worked for Lady Marmalade again. Shortly after this job, the trailer for *Full Love* was released. The movie was renamed *The Eagle Path* and to my delight, they had used my head kick scene in the trailer. They also credited my character in the film as Byron and things were looking up.

TAKE 4

I was invited to audition for two more Indian productions seven days after the Lady Marmalade movie. I was dubious after the last Indian film about health and safety. Although I needed the money and credits, I didn't think I would ever experience a job like the last one. I travelled to the casting with Ron and we contacted the Texan about the audition. The Texan was begging us to get him some work, as he was skint again. So we sent him the details of the films. One of the movies was being filmed on a luxury ship in the Gulf of Thailand and there would be a massive gunfight. The plan was to film a shootout sequence similar to *The Gunfight at the O.K. Corral.* It would be a new experience to film on a ship at sea, which sounded right up my alley. Filming in the lush blue sea and on a plush cruiser linear appealed to me.

A marina near Pattaya was scheduled to host the second production and that sounded appealing. I did my thing again at the audition, a bit of boxing and Thai boxing and they asked me if I could handle and shoot a gun. The film needed a whole team of guys, getting on it wasn't a problem. The Texan attended the casting. Knowing what was coming, I stayed well away. A Thai guy helped him. There was no holding back for the Texan. After walking off bruised, the Thai geezer regretted helping him. The Texan told the casting director that he had 47 street fights again, all won by KO. It seemed like the casting director did not understand what he said, as they looked confused. The Texan was likely trying to boast in order to make himself seem more impressive, but it came off as bragging and was unnecessary. His physical attributes were already enough to make him stand out from the rest and his character face was perfect for a villain role. It was such a shame that a man of his age was so insecure.

While the Texan was performing, another guy showed up. It was the first time I'd seen him; I'll call him the Catalonian. He was a strong-willed Spaniard, an expert in Hapikido and a Spanish bodyguard. The gangster role was perfect for his edgy, rebellious physique and tattoos. His body was like a finely tuned machine, every muscle was perfectly sculpted, like a masterpiece crafted by a skilled artist. He looked like an alien. I watched the Catalonian cast. He performed some sharp Hapkido techniques. His physique and martial arts skills made him the perfect embodiment of a powerful and dangerous gangster.

A week later, a motley crew of 30 Thai, Westerners and Africans were on the way to the location in a convoy of minibuses. The armourer was also in the convoy, with machine guns and pistols in the back of his van. Among our crew were real-life street gangsters, ex-fighters and stuntmen. If the police had pulled us over, they would have probably thought we were on the way to do a hit. The film set was outside Pattaya City. It's known for its beaches, temples and go-go bars. When we arrived at the location, it became clear that the agent had not been honest with us. The boat was in bad shape. It was a derelict, rusty steel ship on a dry dock in a field just off the sea. It looked like the owner had started to build it and gave up as it was half finished. The ship was surrounded by oxidised old scaffolding in a massive, overgrown field with grass as high as your waist. It was like looking at a deserted kingdom, where the ruler abandoned it amid an epic battle, leaving it in ruins. It was more suited to an apocalyptic movie like *Waterworld* or *Mad Max*. It was disappointing. So much for the cruise linear! They probably gave us the bullshit story of the cruise linear so we would do the job!

We were told that we would film on the boat's top deck, there would be a meeting between gangsters and then a rival gang would invade the ship by climbing up the rusty scaffold. Then the shootout starts. Around 10 a.m. the actors and stunt guys queued up for their costumes. The wardrobe gave me a pair of black jeans, a green jacket and a tribal necklace from the back of a pickup truck. It sounds dodgy, I know, like something out of *Only Fools and Horses*, but that was the wardrobe department a Toyota Hi Lux Pick Up. We changed in the field. While changing into my costume, the Indian stunt coordinator approached me and said my role was a henchman. I would be protecting my boss Wesley with Ron and a guy called Arnaud from France on the main deck of the ship. I would be the first to get shot.

A rusty set of steps led us to the boat's top deck. The steps went up 15 feet and were very unstable. Production should have checked the ship's safety but probably didn't, since it was very dodgy. They had placed some old wooden garden furniture on the top deck, where the gangster deal would take place. Those cheeky buggers in the art department got the furniture from the field adjacent to the boat. Up on the main deck, we were at such a high altitude that the view was quite incredible. The Thai coastline could be seen over the ship's side. As I looked at the camera monitors, the top deck looked awesome, even though the boat looked like the sunken Titanic.

Once we started filming, there was a lot of standing, with introduction shots being filmed of us protecting our boss, Wesley. As the camera focused on us, we looked mean and ready for action. The Indian protagonist, Jayam, walked up the ship's steps and onto the top deck, followed by his bodyguard. We would watch them both cautiously and clutch our guns, just like cowboys before a major shootout. Jayam wore a beige Burberry jacket and proudly displayed a horseshoe moustache just like the Texan. Jayam sat at the table with his bodyguard. The dialogue would begin. Jayam asked Wesley, "Give me the goods." Ron put a black duffle bag on the table. He then took a small bag of cocaine from inside the duffle bag for Jayam to test. Then, "Cut!" The scene was reset. We had to do this around half a dozen times, which was straightforward enough, but the temperature exceeded 38 °C, it was hot and sweaty. The sun reflected off the boat's grey steel. We were getting roasted and production hadn't brought sunscreen or umbrellas for us. In between takes, we had nowhere to go except for the captain's bridge. It was sweltering in there too, with no fans and just like an oven. You could boil an egg on that hot steel. There were only a few blue plastic chairs to sit on and they were like gold dust. It was a fight for a chair, just like a game of musical chairs, where one person is always left without a seat when the music stops. The other decks were incomplete and dangerous to walk down, as it was too dark. Parts of the boat were falling apart with decay, so they were no-go zones. Finally, after a few hours we were ready for the *OK Corral* shootout.

Now, sometimes during the day, you obviously need to go for a pee. The film's line producer, Joe, was a stingy bugger. He only hired one toilet for the whole production crew! And it was one of those horrible, smelly plastic Portaloo's you see at music events or building sites. As you can imagine, it soon got filled up and most of the guys started to look for somewhere else to do their business. A film set with a crew of over 80 men will obviously need to relieve themselves when duty calls. Due to the overflowing Portaloo, some of the team started urinating in the field. The locals got pissed off seeing all these Indian guys pissing out in the open with their dicks out. They had a word with the production managers to tell them to stop. We still had around 4 hours left to shoot that day. Joe told everyone they would have to wait for the loo and do it when they returned to their hotel rooms. Some guys thought sod it and still started to pee in the field, ignoring him. Joe got pissed off and threatened to kick them off the job. He then had a stupid brain wave and said we couldn't get off the boat. What happened next was, that the Indian guys started to piss on the second deck of the ship. Shortly afterwards, the word got around and the rest of the guys started to follow and do the same. You couldn't blame them, they needed to piss somewhere. In no time, there were pools of urine on the second deck between the ship's steel bays. It was dark down there, like a sealed sardine can. Since there was no windows and no air entering the room, the urine remained there and didn't evaporate. It was like a rat trap, sealed off and nowhere to escape the heavy air and the pungent smell of piss.

We were supplied with a limited amount of drinking water. As a result, the Indian guys shared each other's bottles. If you would put your bottle down, you would need to watch it like a hawk, as one of the Indians would drink from it. Ultimately, we took a load of bottles, stashed them in the captain's bridge and one of our team members kept an eye on them. They were like gold dust. That night, we were taken back to our hotel rooms. We thought we were getting a 5-star hotel. They put us up in a dingy short-time hotel. If you don't know, a short-time hotel is used by prostitutes to take their customers. Normally, you get your own room on film sets, usually 5-star accommodation. To top it all off, we were told we had to share rooms. The producers were trying to save money, as always. Some of the guys were angry. I didn't mind if we had separate beds. I decided to share with Ron, but the Catalonian wasn't having any of it and said he slept naked. Nobody wanted to share a room with him. We should have all pulled off that trick. The Texan shared with another guy from Africa. After a shower, we all went out and had some Thai food just off the main walking street in the city. We ordered from the restaurant. The Texan looked at the dish list but didn't order anything, we wondered what was up. The Texan then said, "I have no money, I am in dire straits." He put us all on the spot a bit. Then the guy he was sharing a room with, out of kindness of his heart, lent the Texan around 5,000 baht, which is just over 120 quid. The man's generosity surprised all of us. It seemed that the Texan was so relieved to have some money that he left like a shot, without even enjoying the company he was with. That was the last time we saw him that evening. Then he disappeared into the undergrowth of Pattaya's bars and clubs. After eating, we walked back and had an early night. The next day, we were up early at 6.30 a.m. ready to go on set. The Texan appeared exhausted and grumpy. He said, "I didn't sleep all night, because the guy who lent me the money snored all evening. Oh, and there was some loud prostitute next door having sex all night!" The funny thing was his roommate contradicted what the Texan said to us. He told us, "That's bullshit, the Texan didn't get back till 5 a.m. that morning." It reminded me of school children being finicky with each other.

As soon as we arrived at the shooting location. We returned to the bridge area for some shade and waited for our call. After a few minutes of being there, we could smell a terrible stench coming from the second floor of the boat. It was the smell of urine, which had been brewing all night in the heat. It was disgusting. Blue bottles were flying everywhere. To top it off, some of the Indian crew started to pee down there again. The smell got worse after a few hours when more and more guys started pissing down there. It was so severe that it affected our eyes. The smell at this point was unbearable. It was a relief to go out and film our scenes.

While on the captain's bridge, the Texan casually popped

open a couple of Valiums and washed them down with water. To top it off, he said he had run out of money again and was asking more guys on the boat for some cash. I knew he had severe problems. Later in the afternoon, I asked the Catalonian what kind of diet he was on. He told me it was a high-protein diet. He said, "I eat 35 boiled eggs a day!" I found that amazing. It must have taken him ages to boil them and peel the shells, let alone eat them. The local grocer loved him, though her hens hated him. They had to produce 245 eggs a week just to keep the Catalonian happy. Eating all those eggs was like a religion for him, a way of life. Interesting enough, the organic man from Catalonia was there with natural muscles from egg protein, whereas the Texan was using synthetic injectable testosterone. Excessive testosterone can lead to aggressive and irritable behaviour and sleep apnea, both of which the Texan had. Obviously, it wasn't an ideal situation.

The two were Alpha males, a bit hot-headed and were cramped together, trying to get shade in a small space on the captain's bridge, which wasn't a good thing. The Catalonian and the Texan got talking about diets. The Texan talked about steroids and human growth hormone and the conversation led to fights. The Catalonian spoke about his bodyguarding, Hapikido, Vale Tudo and Muay Thai experience. The Texan spoke about his exploits in life, from diving to Krav Maga to shooting wild boars. It was like two roosters in a barnyard, puffing up their chests and strutting around, trying to one-up each other in a show of dominance. The conversation moved on to what fighting techniques they could use and what worked best. The Texan boasted yet again that he had a baffling 47 registered street fights. After 30 minutes, the Catalonian and the Texan slowly demonstrated techniques to each other. They demonstrated punches, kicks, elbows and how to evade and deflect them. Then it progressed to grappling. It was as if they were trying to prove to each other who was tougher and had more experience in a physical altercation. This led to the conversation focusing on the different types of techniques both knew. They demonstrated these techniques to each other, showing their respective martial arts proficiency.

I could see what was coming next and we all looked on in amusement. The problem with the Texan was that he went in hard again. It started slowly but ended up in a spiral of violence. The Texan was too proud to tap out and kept fighting his way out of the locks and arm bars. He was too aggressive, it ended in a physical altercation. The Catalonian had the upper hand and the Texan was on the brink of losing consciousness due to a sleeper headlock. The Texan's head looked like it was bursting like a squashed tomato and he wouldn't tap. The Texan tried to push the Catalonian back against the steel wall by trying to get up and pushing him back with his legs. As a result, the Texan nearly split his own head open as it hit the steel wall. We calmed the situation down and they were separated. It was quite an eventful afternoon. They didn't talk much after that.

When it was time for filming, we were called back onto the deck by one of the Indian coordinators. He didn't have a clue what took place inside the bridge. The Indian coordinator told me a sniper would shoot me in the neck. They would place a squib on my jacket collar. Once it went off, I had to react and fall to the floor. When they fixed my squib, I checked it for a plate. The steel plate protects the actor from the force of the charge, while the fake blood packet provides a realistic visual effect. The squib itself is designed to be as safe as possible, with its charge strong enough to break the fake blood packet and rip the actor's clothing but not strong enough to injure the actor. The pyro guys carefully attached the squib to my jacket collar. The squib was live and ready to go, we went to our positions. Guns were locked and loaded and safety catches were engaged. As our bosses sat at the table, we protected them. All their flanks were covered.

We formed a staggered V formation, with Ron beside me and the Texan in front of us. We were told by the coordinator that a group of gunmen would invade the ship after the main lead actor got up and started shooting. We would be taken out one by one by snipers and those invading the ship. After I fired my pistol four times, the stunt coordinator told me a sniper on a crane would take me out. Then Ron would be shot, the Texan would flee with the mob boss to the back of the boat and be shot in the shoulder by the Catalonian. For obvious reasons, the Catalonian loved the idea of shooting the Texan in the back. Everyone else remaining on the deck would be shot by the invading gunman and Jayam. After 20 minutes, we were ready to proceed. Guns were locked and loaded and the Indian version of the *OK Corral* shootout was about to start. The action director called, "Ready! Ready! ACTION!"

All hell broke loose, gunfire came from all directions.

Empty, hot bullet shells flew everywhere at 45 degrees and hit us. It was then that I realised we were too close together. It was a good thing we had earplugs. I fired my pistol four times, shooting directly over the ship's stern at a sniper on a crane opposite and then, BANG! My squib exploded. I felt a rush of warm fake blood explode on my neck. I reacted and collapsed on the steel floor. I hit the boat's steel deck with a heavy thump! The gunfight lasted for a few minutes. I kept my head down and my eyes closed as empty, hot, smoking 9-mm shells landed on my face. Blank bullet shells flew everywhere like hailstones. The sound of the gunfight was deafening and unending. It was almost surreal as I lay there, listening to the sound of shells hitting the steel deck and feeling the heat coming off them as they flew by. The scene only ended when the director called "CUT!"

I got up, dusted myself down and waited. The armourer came over and was smiling like a Cheshire cat. He gave us more bullets to load into our magazines and put them in our pistols. He noted in his notepad with a big smile how many blanks he gave us. Meanwhile, the director checked the takes. He wanted to make sure everyone was in sync when the squibs went off. This was critical to ensuring the action sequences looked realistic and that all the actors were reacting properly to the shots. Immediately, the pyro guys came up to me, took the old, exploded squib out of my jacket and added a new one to it. An Indian tailor came over and sewed the hole up where the explosion ripped my coat from the squib. I thought they would give me another jacket, but they only had one.

The tailor used a wet sponge to wipe the blood off the

jacket. Then he wiped the blood from my neck and I was ready to go. The scene was reset and we attempted another shot. We staggered our formation this time instead of standing side-by-side, therefore the hot shells wouldn't hit us. We went for a second take. Everyone's timing was perfect. I shot my pistol four times, the squib exploded. My body fell to the hot steel floor. Again, I lay on the deck without moving, waiting for, "Cut." To be called. My job was over. My fellow gangsters and I lay in a pool of fake blood on the hot steel deck for the rest of the day. I gained an intense suntan. There was such happiness in the armourer's eyes. Considering that he charged $5 per bullet, he made a killing! The other scenes were filmed while we lay in the afternoon sun, playing dead. For continuity, they needed us there again. It was a strange experience, as the environment was quite different from the previous one, yet the same type of scene was being filmed. This time though, the sun shone down on me. Instead of river water, I had a swarm of blue bottles feasting on fake blood on my neck. It almost felt like a different world, yet it was the same job as before.

The lack of basic creature comforts on set was indicative of the disregard that producers had for the action performers, who were seen as expendable and replaceable. The lack of showers and other amenities, coupled with having to wash off fake blood with bottles of water, was a reminder of this reality. It was a source of frustration for the performers. I wanted better roles than this. Some performers may grumble about the grueling conditions on other film shoots, but they have yet to experience the truly absurd demands of the sets I have worked on. But such challenges are minor in comparison to the demands of a construction site. I had been lying on the ground in my last few movies, shot or beaten, but I figured I needed to start somewhere.

The Jean-Claude film proved to be a promising beginning, but I sensed the need to elevate my craft as similar movies were not appearing with sufficient frequency. I set out to enhance my approach. Lying there in that heat on the top deck of that shipwreck inspired me to try harder. I didn't want to become cannon fodder and I knew I had more to offer. I intended to do some crazy death scenes that people would remember me for and of course, I really wished to do some dialogue! I knew working on these types of films was short-lived. Eventually, I would have given up if they were the only roles I landed. I wanted to move on to bigger and better things. It's funny how the universe works sometimes. Things were going to get extremely busy for me.

The following week, we shot at the marina for the second Indian movie. We were gangsters again and confronted a rival gang. Yet again, there were no mats to fall on. As with the other chaps, I got killed again and fell to the hard concrete floor. A pattern was forming. It was the fourth time this had happened. I had gotten proficient at bullet hits and dying at this point. My timing was spot on! Even though it was hard to fall on those concrete and steel floors, the crash course in dying would help me with future projects. A smooth sea never makes a skilled sailor. In life, you have to take the good with the bad. I was lying on the ground, looking at the stars. The cool thing about this film production was that they were cheating the location for Monaco, I wish I had been there then. Little did I know that a few years later, I would get booked on a TV series filming at the millionaire's playground. The path to success isn't always smooth and sometimes you have to pass through difficult times to reach your goals.

Unfortunately, during the last days of this job, some low-life thieves stole money from one of the stunt guys' wallets. The stunt guy left his wallet on the minibus for safekeeping with his other belongings. The only person who had access to the bus was the driver. When the stunt guy returned from the shoot, he found that his wallet had quite a few notes taken from it. Joe didn't want to hear it. He thought we were trying to pull a fast one. Ultimately, he blacklisted us from his productions and did us a favour. We were all growing within the industry and going on to better things. Despite the poor conditions, I got some good footage for my showreel, which was my main goal. After that job, Joe started using cheap labour. Remember, moviemaking is a business, producers want the most cost-effective deal. He began using eastern European extras as action guys at a quarter of our price. As with everything in life, you get what you pay for. I soon learned someone was always waiting to jump into your shoes in the film industry and work for peanuts. As a result, Joe's productions suffered from a lack of quality and professionalism. He was taking a short-term approach to cutting costs by using cheaper extras, but the quality of his productions suffered due to a lack of experienced talent and the inability to provide them with the necessary resources to do their job properly.

If you are an ex-pat, there is no unemployment benefit. You either run your own business or have a second income. You are on your own. There is only backup if you have lots of savings. It's like being in a jungle, with no safety net, you must do whatever it takes to survive, but the resources are limited and you need to be able to outcompete the other animals in order to get ahead. I learned that many guys who work on film productions work on whatever movie comes up, because they have no choice. Many were trapped in that lifestyle. Some were so desperate they even did porn! They had families and no other financial backup. It caused friction in the industry as producers and agents played off that. Some agents knew they had many guys by the balls. This created a vicious cycle of dishonesty and desperation. Some Individuals were willing to do the job for less money and those with more skills were unable to compete. This reduced the overall quality of the work being done, as producers and agents were more likely to go with the lowest bidder instead of the most qualified individual. For now, these films were a good access point to bigger and better productions. Soon though it was time to move on.

TAKE 5

The day had come to begin to work on *Largo Winch 2*, also known as the Burma Conspiracy. The French action thriller *Largo Winch* is based on the Belgian comic book series by Phillipe Francq and Jean Van Hamme. It was an exciting opportunity to work on a project that had a global fan base. The film not only gave me a chance to work in an international environment, but it also gave me an opportunity to work with some of the most talented people in the film industry. It was also a chance to gain more autonomy and develop my skills in a new role. The first day I was introduced to our team at Don Mueang airport, where we were going to shoot a scene leaving our private jet. They had some very talented stunt performers on this one. The French stunt coordinator was Philippe Guegan, who has over 340 credits to his name. They had Jerome Gaspard, who is well-known in the stunt industry and has a wealth of experience. They also had Seng from Seng Stunts. Seng is also a highly respected coordinator, especially for Thai stunt crews. We had some of the top stunt performers in the industry and I was excited to work with them. I knew this would be a fantastic experience and I couldn't wait to start.

I met our Serbian mercenary team. The mercenaries were picked for their expertise in their respective fields. Our leader, Clemens Shick, played Dragan. He is best known for his role as Kraat in James Bond's *Casino Royale*. Sebastien Vandenberghe was another great guy I met over 6 feet tall, bulging muscles and a true powerhouse with lightning elbows and reactions. He worked on *Taken* and *The Transporter*. He was one of the top instructors of the lethal MDS fighting system. The outstanding and tough-as-nails Olivia Jackson added some femininity to the team. Olivia was a former fighter at the Kaesermerit Muay Thai gym in Bangkok. She kicked hard like a baseball bat. Adding to the flavour was the world's highest kicker, Ron Smoorenburg. With his pinpoint kicks, Ron is best known for playing in Jackie Chan's film, *Who Am I?* To be honest, we look cool. Together, the team created a formidable force that impressed on screen. They had matched us perfectly.

We all got along so well from the start and remain good friends today. We all shared a common goal and had a deep passion for what we were doing, which created a powerful bond between us. We also had a strong sense of camaraderie, which made us work better together. It was one of those times when it was like we had known each other for years but hadn't. The first scene to be filmed was a walking shot of our team entering and leaving a green private jet bearing the Winch Air logo. It took around 3 hours to get the right shot. The picture of five of us Serbian mercenaries walking across the tarmac in full combat gear with weapon bags was awesome. The second scene we filmed was us bad guys on the private jet. This shot was used to establish the stakes of the mission and create a sense of urgency and tension in the audience. This heightened the anticipation for the forthcoming fight scene and gave the audience an insight into the characters motivations. As you know, I had not spoken in any of the films I had been in at the time. I was inspired by Clemens Schick's performance as Dragan. There was something natural about him, less was more. I was really inspired to try and get dialogue roles from watching him. I saw how natural and authentic Clemens performance was and how he conveyed so much emotion with just a few words. This made me realise that I could do the same in the right roles. I didn't need to rely on big, showy performances to make an impact. The second day we were filming in downtown Bangkok and then it was up to the jungles of the north.

Most of the shooting for *Largo Winch 2* was done in Mae Hong Son. This was done with some stints in Chiang Mai and of course, Bangkok. The crew chose this location because of the stunning visuals and the unique atmosphere it provided for the film. The jungle setting was perfect for the story, the lush landscape was ideal for capturing the many action sequences. They built a village and prison cells from scratch. The crew also added authentic props and decorations to give the set an even more realistic feel. They used actual Burmese military uniforms and weapons, as well as other items such as typical furniture and cooking utensils. Filmmaking is not just about actors who bring the film to life but also set builders, art departments, writers and directors. The result was an extremely realistic and believable set, which captured the audience's attention and enhanced the story. It was a true testament to all the departments hard work and dedication. The attention to detail in the set design and the collaboration between the various departments allowed the story to be brought to life. This would not have been possible with just one or two creative minds. Each person brings their own unique skills and perspective to the project, which creates a more dynamic and engaging result.

Away from the film set, they set up a canteen area, tents, restrooms and a stunt training area in the jungle, which was matted out. That was awesome to see. Stunt teams would practice their techniques throughout the day. The base camp was an ideal way for the crew to bond and work together. The stunt training area allowed them to practice and perfect their stunts. It was a fantastic experience to be part of a production that was so organised and dedicated to creating an excellent movie. On my first day I got to fly in a Huey helicopter, from the Vietnam War. It had served in the war for several years and had been used in numerous missions, including search and rescue, medical evacuation and transporting military personnel and supplies. The Thai military refurbished it for drug patrols. It was an amazing experience to fly in such a machine with so much history. It was used by our mercenary team to hunt *Largo Winch* in the film. It was truly breathtaking to soar through the lush green jungle, taking in the vastness of the landscape and the beauty of the nature below. The feeling of freedom and adventure was unparalleled. As we sat in the helicopter, armed with machine guns, we looked pretty cool. There was quite a bit of time spent flying around until the perfect shot was taken.

While flying, Dragan gets a garrote and strangles the corrupt Burmese General Kyaw Min. The general is thrown out of the helicopter and falls to the ground. The scene was meant to depict Dragan's power and strength and how they could take down their enemies in a single, swift move. After watching the tourniquet performance, I was inspired to do my fight scene. Filming would take place in a studio called Moonstar Studios.

A few weeks later, we began training for the fight with Mr. Largo Winch. The first time I went to the studio, I was blown away by what they created. The set designers created a replica of the Winch Air private jet, complete with the same features and details as a real jet. This jet was mounted on a hydraulic platform. This platform was designed to simulate the physical sensations of being on a plane. This includes the acceleration of takeoff, the swaying of turbulence and the dropping sensation of a plane. It took around one week to train for the fight scene. With Philippe overseeing the action, Jerome and an assistant named Thierry Saelens taught us. In addition to being very enthusiastic, Thierry had a lot of passion for what he was doing. We trained every day until we mastered the choreography. So here is the basic breakdown of what we needed to film. On the jet, a major fight breaks out between the mercenary team, *Largo Winch* and his assistant Simon. In the chaos of the fight, Simon manages to open the door of the plane, causing a sudden drop in air pressure. This makes it difficult to breathe and causes objects to be sucked out of the plane. With the sudden decompression, Largo takes advantage of the situation and jumps out of the plane, with Dragan in pursuit.

I had the pleasure of watching Olivia Jackson and

It Ain't All Glitz & Glamour

Sebastien Vandenberghe in action one day on the set. There was a major fight scene with Largo Winch, Sebastien and Olivia. I was blown away by their talent and how seamlessly they worked together as a team. They turned a simple scene into an unforgettable moment on screen. Their chemistry was undeniable, it was obvious they had a deep understanding of their characters. I felt like I was watching a *Jason Bourne* movie. At that point, I realised how talented these actresses and stuntmen were by doing scenes in one continuous take. Most western movies show the action close-up, or from an angle because the actors sometimes cannot perform the action. One continuous take is very rare in the Hollywood film industry. In many films, they shoot from behind or from an angle so that they can use stunt doubles, as many actors cannot perform action sequences. Working in Asia allowed me to be immersed in a different culture with its own unique ways of approaching action scenes. This gave me an opportunity to observe and learn from different types of actors and directors that I may not have had the chance to work with in the West. That's one thing I like about the guys I met in Thailand. Many of the guys can act and do stunts and they are bloody good at it.

The next morning, we worked through the blocking, which is the positioning of actors and cameras for the scene. To simulate decompression after the emergency door opens, the crew placed massive fans at each end of the plane. While we were inside, they tested the fans and turned them on. The wind pressure was so strong that it generated enough force to lift objects off the ground and made it difficult to stay on your feet. It was like an invisible hand pushing everything away, making it impossible to resist its force. The challenge of filming a fight scene in such conditions was thrilling and unique. Once all safety checks were completed, we were ready to film.

We took our positions. The director called, "Action!" We took Largo Winch from the captain's cockpit at gunpoint. Dragan pushed Largo to the back of the plane and I kneed him in the stomach. Turning him around, I locked him in a hammer lock. He struggled and he tried to fight back. I tightened my grip. Dragan then punched Largo in the face and stomach. Then Simon, Largo's copilot, came out of the cockpit and tried to hit Ron with a fire extinguisher. In response to the commotion near the cockpit, Dragan left Largo in my hands and I pushed Largo down onto a seat. Dragan then threatened Simon with his gun during the commotion. This situation was like a game of chess, with each character making a move to gain the upper hand. The gun was Dragan's checkmate, forcing Simon to take the only action left to him in order to escape. Simon pulled the emergency exit lever, opening the door. Then "Cut!" was called.

All takes were checked and everything was fine. The final instalment of the fight scene was followed by a short break. The assistant called us back to our last position. The crew turned on the fans they had placed at each corner of the fuselage. The fans created a powerful and intense wind effect that made it seem like the air pressure was so strong it could rip the plane apart. This added to the tension and danger of the scene and created an atmosphere of impending doom. The powerful wind gave a feeling of reality to the scene. The director called "Action!" We went for it with all the energy we had. I hit Largo Winch with my right elbow dozens of times on his shoulder. I then pushed him onto a seat still in the hammer lock and he fell. Trying to free himself, he reached under the seat for an emergency parachute. Since everything was flying around in the fuselage, he grabbed a tray and hit me with it, knocking me out. He then jumped out of the plane with a parachute. Immediately behind him was Dragan. Talk about a dramatic exit! Now you're probably wondering how Largo Winch got out of the plane. In this sequence, they did some film trickery, attaching a cable to Largo Winch and pulling him out of the air when he was near the emergency exit. The cable was removed during post-production.

That scene took 13 hours to shoot. It was a long and exhausting day. Even though the scene took a long time to film, the crew managed to capture all the intricate details and make it look as realistic as possible. It was a fantastic experience for everyone involved and it showed how much hard work and dedication is put into creating a movie. It was like a marathon runner's grueling race. However, at the finish line, there was a feeling of accomplishment and joy to be shared in the celebration of a beer. That night, I returned home a happy man, proud of my achievements. We had a few days of rest before flying to Belgium.

After a few days of waiting for our flight to Belgium, Ron got a call from another production. He was asked if he knew of three menacing guys who would be interested in playing gangsters in a film called *Elephant White*. So, Ron put me and the Texan forward for the job. He thought that our combined skills and experience would make us the right candidates for the film. After the piss boat job, we gave the Texan the benefit of the doubt and gave him another chance because he needed money. This opened another adventure for us.

The scene we were booked into involved gangsters running with guns to protect our boss. Even though it was just a small, featured role, I thought, why not? I would gain an insight into the creative process of two very talented actors, Kevin Bacon, who played Jimmy and Djimon Hounsou, who played Curtie. For any actor or director who aspires to be a part of this industry, this would be invaluable. Furthermore, it would be an honour to be part of such a prestigious production and see two of the most iconic actors of our generation. The opportunity to gain experience, meet stars and make valuable connections appealed to me.

The production asked us if we didn't mind bringing our own suits, if possible, just in case they didn't have our sizes. I knew the other guys would most likely be dressed in black, I wanted to make sure I was noticed and remembered. I figured that by wearing a light grey suit, I would stand out from the rest and be more memorable. We were told what we were going to do in the film. The assistant director explained, "Curtie drives his Mercedes through a wall and shoots at the bodyguards. Your boss is then confronted by him, you have to defend your boss." For us, it was just a few running shots inside the mansion with guns and a few scenes with Jimmy the Brit and Curtie. I really wanted to be in the same scene as these guys. Several parts of our scene were choreographed by the stunt team. In the action department, everything is broken down and edited together to create a masterpiece. The first part of the sequence was the car driving into the mansion wall. The scene was carefully choreographed by the stunt team. It was timed so that Curtie's entrance would be perfectly in sync with our bodyguards at the mansion. We were ready to act instantly when the car crashed through the wall to protect our boss. Now, to let you guys know, obviously the wall was a fake wall. How they made it was by using 8 by 4 polystyrene sheets. The wall was then cleverly disguised with paint and wallpaper to blend in with the rest of the mansion. This made it almost impossible to distinguish it from the real wall.

Finally, the car crashed into the wall and the scene was complete. The next scene was us bodyguards running through the mansion after the car crashed through the wall. One American guy who was playing one of the bodyguards ran alongside me as we ran through the massive mansion. He was a bloater and I couldn't believe how unfit he was. He struggled to keep up with the rest of us. His breathing was like that of a broken engine, sputtering and stalling as he desperately tried to keep up. Within an hour or so, we got the shot and then it was on to the next scene, which would have a lot of standing and pointing guns. On the last shot of the evening, the set was rearranged and then it was onto the main scene with Jimmy the Brit and Curtie. The scene was thrilling, with intense action and suspense. We were there with around 20 bodyguards with guns pointing at Curtie. He held our boss at gunpoint. Jimmy the Brit walked towards our mob boss and the negotiations began. It was an exciting moment to be part of a scene with two big Hollywood actors. It was amazing to be so closely connected to them in the film. Observing two acclaimed actors working together was a fantastic opportunity. It was an invaluable experience that I will never forget.

As the actors did their dialogue, we were standing about 20 feet away, pointing guns at them. This was fortunate because the American stomach made strange sounds. I could hear this American's stomach rumbling like Mount Kilimanjaro. It was embarrassing. While working alongside these icons, I thought don't fart mate. The ripper would have picked up on the sound. Fortunately, the American was able to control his digestion and the shots were successful. The actors were able to deliver their lines without interruption and the American's stomach held back until the takes were finished. After that, we kept our distance from him. We worked all night to get the perfect scene and then we were booked for a few more days shooting at the international airport.

The Texan didn't get used again, because he had upset the main producer of the film. Shooting at the airport was a lot of fun. There was a lot of running around looking for Curtie. We were weaving in and out of extras while getting into and out of black Mercedes cars, like mafia hitmen. At times there was an audience from the public, which was cool. I spoke to Djimon during the day, we talked about all sorts of subjects and the funny thing was that we shared a common friend. Djimon and I were amazed to discover that the friend, we had in common was someone we both had a history with at very different points in our lives. During our conversation, I mentioned a guy named John Mundy from Kent who had seen a photo of me and Djimon together on Facebook. John wanted to be remembered to him. To cut a long story short, in the 1980s, I followed quite a few street punk bands all around the UK. John was the vocalist for one of them. Djimon told me he knew John from doing the doors in Los Angeles and they were mates. I think the sixth degree of Kevin Bacon was working here. It's a fascinating example of how small our world really is and how interconnected we all are.

Now I'd like to explain a small trick I played on *Elephant White*. Despite my small part and featured extra role, you only see me for a few seconds. I made the most of it. I used this film to book other jobs. I had a strategy in mind. By wearing a grey suit, I made a statement that I was different from other actors wearing black suits and that my character was more significant. Even though my character wasn't. I knew that the grey suit would be a subtle way to draw attention to my character. No matter what I did, I always stuck to my plan to get noticed, especially in these small roles. I understood that even in minor roles, if I had a few unique features that stood out, that could be the difference between being noticed and not. The grey suit was a way of showcasing my character without being too showy. I trusted my instincts and they were proven correct when I got a call back for another film. This was after another director saw me in *Elephant White* two years later. It's not enough to be good, you must leave an impression. To make an impact, you must be unique and be memorable, you need something that makes you stand out from the competition. The grey suit was a subtle way of doing that and it worked. It's like putting a bow on a present it doesn't change the gift, but it dresses it up and brings attention to it.

In the following days, I flew to Belgium to complete the scenes for *Largo Winch 2*. A shooting day took place at an airport in Belgium. After walking away from our Winch air jet with automatic weapons in our bags, Ron and I get arrested at the airport. It was cool to be in this scene with *Basic Instinct* star Sharon Stone. This scene was key to the movie's plot, as it set up the climax and showed the audience that the bad guys had been taken down. Unlike many other movies, I survived this one without dying! After working on these cool films with iconic Hollywood stars, my plan was starting to work. Though my contribution to *Largo Winch 2* was small, success came from taking small steps and I was earning credits. Afterwards, I flew to England to talk to a few agents. I returned to Thailand, where I had auditions scheduled for three movies and many TV commercials, all with speaking roles. As a result, I felt more confident than ever before. I was sure I would make a name for myself in the industry. I was looking forward to the challenge. I was optimistic that, together with my newfound experience and skills, I could secure at least one of the roles. Maintaining a training routine helped me stay focused and take advantage of opportunities.

With my experience on various film sets, I landed more television commercials and eventually worked on an international television series. I got booked on a Korean TV drama called *City Hunter*. As well I was scheduled for jobs in India. It didn't matter what came my way, I took it. It was like a snowball rolling down a mountain, the more I trained and worked, the more opportunities were presented to me and the bigger my career grew. I attended five different castings for five different movies to be filmed over the course of a year. It was very important to me at this point to land a speaking role, I did my best to land one. The movies were *The Mark, Vikingdom, The Hangover Part 2, Sming* and *Only God Forgives.*

TAKE 6

The Mark was a thriller movie starring Eric Roberts and Gary Daniels from *The Expendables*. The audition details for this movie caught my attention immediately. There were quite a few similarities between it and the *Largo Winch* 2 movie. The character I was casting for was Jenson, a paramilitary soldier. There would be a scene where I and a group of guys hijack a plane. I was confident that I could handle the action and dialogue required for the role. Being an ideal match for the position, I knew I could make an impression with the few lines I had. For me, this was a cross-over point since I had spent many hours on many sets, but none with dialogue. It was where I wanted to be in the film industry, acting and doing some action. Each new experience I had in the film industry contributed to the larger picture I was creating for myself. Every piece of the puzzle brought me one step closer to achieving my goal.

The first day on set, we were informed that an American evangelical Christian film production were producing this film. They had a massive catalogue of films behind them and they hadn't lost any money on any of their previous films. We were told there would be no swearing in the film whatsoever. This company was successful because they had a niche audience. They created films that appealed to their audience without alienating viewers with too much violence or bad language. My character's name in *The Mark* was Jenson. He was a skilled mercenary and the right-hand man of the film's main protagonist, Joseph Pike. I would have lots of good scenes to shoot, this was very important to me. Considering Eric Roberts had just completed *The Expendables* and was an iconic actor, the footage would be golden. Being associated with actors of this type was beneficial to my career. I was in the right place at the right time.

They had built the plane from plywood and fiberglass in a studio on Bangkok's outskirts. It was impressive how they managed to put this one together, as it was different from the *Largo Winch* plane. By having a stationary platform, they could remove the seats and the sides of the plane, which allowed them to get the camera angles they wanted. This allowed them to shoot scenes inside without having to move the entire plane around, which could have been difficult and expensive. I had one scene when I was planting the bomb on the cockpit door. The props department gave me a cool fake bomb. They made it out of shower gel bottles with blue and green shower gel inside. It had a battery and an electronic timer with wires attached. It was the perfect prop for the scene, as it provided the necessary visual effect without costing too much.

My dialogue scenes were easy and I nailed it. I had practiced my lines beforehand and was familiar with the characters and the setting. It was like taking a small dip in a lake before jumping into the deep end. It was a great way to get used to the water, before tackling the more challenging task of what was to come later in my filming career.

Like all the villains in movies, we all have an unfortunate ending and this film was no different. We bad guys have bombs, we have big guns and yet we all seem to get taken out, by one bullet by a pretty guy with a small gun! I suppose the audience loves a bit of fantasy! I would like to do a film one day where the hero gets taken out and leaves the audience gobsmacked just for the unexpected shock factor. I would get shot and fall through a glass partition on the plane. Because they fitted me with two squibs, it was going to be quite an involved operation and a very entertaining death scene. Therefore, I was looking forward to it immensely. I would run through the plane like a madman with the bomb in my hand. I would then try and shoot Chad Turner, the hero of the movie. I would be shot by Chad in the chest. The second squib would go off on my back, splattering the window behind me. As I get shot, I throw the bomb at Chad. The bomb gets chucked down the garbage chute by Chad, it explodes and the plane crashes, however like all heroes Chad escapes. This only works in action movies folks!

The death scene was shot in two set-ups. One continuous take was used for the first set-up. I had some dialogue with my boss Joseph Pike, then we find out one of our men is missing. I ran through the aircraft with the bomb and gun in hand. The passengers scream and Eric Roberts hid, as I marched past him like a man possessed. It was like a roller coaster ride, with moments of terror and excitement. I felt adrenaline coursing through my veins as I ran through the plane. I knew I had to act quickly and precisely for the shot to succeed. To accomplish this, they took the sides of the plane

It Ain't All Glitz & Glamour

away and recorded a tracking shot of me. The tracking shot was a clever way to create danger and suspense. As I approached the glass partition, I saw Chad Turner, the hero, crouching on the ground and pointing his gun at me. "Cut!" Was called. I got to the scene in two takes and it was time to move on.

My glass smash scene was about to begin. Two squibs were fitted to me by the stunt coordinator and the pyro guys, one on my chest and another at the back of my jacket. The devices were going to be activated remotely. They only had a few sheets of breakaway glass for this scene, I had to get it right. Sugar glass sheets are very expensive and you can't mess up. If I didn't get the shot right, they wouldn't be able to use it in the film, so the pressure was on me. They placed two small explosive charges at the corners of the glass, making it easier to shatter. As soon as I pointed the gun at Chad, my chest and back squibs would explode. Within seconds, the glass partition would shatter. This had to be done at the exact moment I pointed the gun at Chad, otherwise, the effect wouldn't have been as convincing. Timing was crucial and I could not make mistakes. They only had a limited amount of time to pull this off if I got it wrong, it would take at least an hour to reinstall the window and clean up.

I rehearsed this scene repeatedly, memorising every detail, to ensure my timing was perfect. It took careful precision and preparation between me and the stunt coordinator. Even the slightest mistake could have ruined the entire scene. My safety gear included a turtle back to protect my spine and I had knee guards and elbow pads.

The coordinator demonstrated that the best way to break the glass. I was given a stuntman's tip that day. He said, "It's always a wise safety precaution to crack sugar glass with your elbow before passing through it, so your body doesn't take the full impact."

I was ready for my death scene once I reverted to my original position. As Chad was crouching in front of me, I pointed my gun at him. After giving the coordinator the nod, the stunt coordinator called out, "Action!" Adrenaline shot through my body and it felt great. It was like being hit with a jolt of electricity that gave me a surge of energy. I fired my gun and the squib went off on my chest. I reacted to it and within seconds, the second squib went off on my shoulder, I reacted again. After stumbling for a few seconds, I threw the bomb at Chad. Upon falling backwards, I slammed my elbows against the breakaway glass to smash it. The glass's charges exploded upon impact. As my elbows crushed against the glass partition, there was a loud cracking sound as the glass cracked. It was at this point that I relaxed my body and let gravity do the rest. I fell to the floor with my arms wide open, spreading the impact all over the floor. My body was covered with millions of glass shards. I lay there, unable to move, in a pool of blood, feeling victorious. It was like I was lying in a bed of diamonds, each one a memory of my victory. I knew I did a great job!

I was left with my fate sealed in a puddle of blood as the dust settled. I was dead on the floor after another dramatic ending. My skills at dying were getting better and better! As if I were playing a game of death repeatedly, every death and explosion became more elaborate and daring. It took them five minutes to clean the sugar glass shards from my face and clothes. I watched the scene. Everyone was delighted that I was able to get the scene in one take! It was my first ever glass smash! All in all, I was proud of myself and was enthusiastic to continue playing and perfecting my death scene skills.

In a conversation with one of the main actors on *The Mark*, I mentioned to him, he might be able to get a lot of work in Thailand. He said to me, "Whatever you do, don't get labelled as a local Byron." This resonated with me. This comment made me realise that it was imperative to consider the implications of being viewed as a local. It also made me realise that I should aim to be cast as an international actor even more, so that I would have more opportunities to work outside Thailand. Actors who are seen as locals are paid less for their roles, which limits their earning potential. I didn't want to be restricted to a certain region or country. I knew it was essential to look for more global opportunities to expand my career. I wanted to use the credits I was accumulating to get them. I had many other projects looming after this film. One was in Malaysia and I was determined to get them all. Thailand was bustling with movies at the time and I had the chance to cast for *The Hangover Part 2*.

The film was all the rage when it came to town. Most of the roles were cast in the United States. Expats were to cast for the leftovers. Despite auditioning for a small role, I wasn't successful, they wanted a different type of character look, than the one I auditioned for. I wasn't going to let that stop me. Determined, I thought of a different angle to get into the movie and headed down another route.

I contacted the film's Thai stunt coordinator. He was familiar with my work. There was a bar fight scene where they needed a few guys to fight Bradley Cooper, Ed Helms and Zach Galifianakis. Again, this was right up my street, even though there were no lines, it was still an opportunity to get seen in the movie. I jumped at the chance to be in the film. I loved the first one and who wouldn't want to be in *The Hangover*? I knew the movie would have a large audience. Being associated with the movie would give me a platform to be seen and noticed by casting directors.

The American stunt coordinator, Allan Graf had a brilliant CV of hundreds of films, including *Pirates of the Caribbean, Bad Santa* and *The Dark Knight*. Working under him was going to be an honour. It had been a while since I'd seen The Texan, but he showed up at the casting. He was desperate and asked me for money, which I declined. He asked a stupid and embarrassing question when we were being interviewed by Allan. He said, "Who's going to supply the safety gear?" Allan was dumbfounded when he was asked that question, the rest of us wondered what planet the Texan was on. Allan ripped into him. I felt like crawling under a table. If you work in the stunt industry or as an actor who works on action films, it is essential that you have your own safety gear. Without them, you're like a builder without tools. So, I kept my distance from the Texan, as I didn't want to be associated with him.

I was confirmed on the job. Filming took place off a seedy street. No matter what you are looking for, you can find it somewhere on that road. With new signs, the production renamed some of the bars and took over the whole street.

It Ain't All Glitz & Glamour

That evening, we were told to meet at the base camp, opposite the shooting location, which was an empty plot of land next to the Sky train stop. The director and the stunt coordinator showed up. The director picked me and Ron as the guys he wanted in the bar to fight the main actors. We were then escorted by one of the coordinators to a waiting area, which was a bar inside the street. It was an interesting situation, some of the bars were still open for business. It was almost surreal to have ladies of the night trying to sell their services to us while we waited to shoot. It was certainly an eye-opening and comical experience. One of the ladies asked one of our guys, "Would you like a blowjob before you go to work?" he laughed it off. The rumour on the street was that Bill Clinton was in town that night. Apparently, he was going to do a cameo role in the film. But I never saw him!

I had a conversation with the Mamasan of the bar we waited in, she proudly told me who her highest-performing employees were. Gold badges were worn by some of the ladies, including a ladyboy. Badges were awarded for their accomplishments. It was like a competition between two athletes, it was like a badge of honour. The average number of customers per shift for a gold badge holder was 20. She explained to me that the badge signified that the customer was getting the finest service possible. It was common for customers to seek out gold badge holders for their services, since they were the most experienced. It was like a reward system, not only for employees but also for customers. In the bar, every girl had sponsors from around the globe. It was common for women to earn as much as 6,000 pounds a month just from all their boyfriends. Many had at least four guys on the go. Every girl would have a birthday every month, so the customer had to pay for the entire bar.

The Mamasan was candid about it all. It was an eye-opening night for me, regarding the brothel industry. After a few hours of waiting in the bar, we were taken to the shooting location. The location was three doors down and the owner was an Englishman. As we waited inside to shoot, the owner told me he was selling up after the film finished. He was very happy. He must have been making so much money from the movie that he decided to call it a day. We were left in the bar alone for an hour or so, to work on choreography that could be used in the scene. Shortly afterwards, the props department started laying out breakaway glass bottles in the bar area. They told me and Ron which ones were made from sugar glass, so we knew where to fall. We had a safety meeting with the team, then it was time to shoot.

The main cast walked in. Ed Healms was a cool guy, very funny. Bradley Cooper was chilled and was also very pleasant to talk to. As we sat at the bar, Zach however, didn't say a word. The director explained to me and Ron what he wanted in the scene. He said, "The cast will be drinking at the bar, including the monk with the monkey. Ron and you are drunk, Bradley walks over to the bar and orders a drink. As he does, he spills a drink on you. You then turn around and push Bradley back. He throws a big punch at you, knocking you to the ground. A few seconds later, all cast members will jump on top of you. Punching, kicking and abusing you. Ron will also be jumped upon by the crowd, after he is thrown to the ground. So you have to react quickly and safely. Not only that, but we will have to do it, with both the adult cast and the younger cast. There will be a crazy flashback scene using this sequence."

They brought in many extras for this scene. Some came from the Khaosan Road backpacker neighbourhood. There were quite a few hippies in the bar at the time. When it was time to shoot the first take, everyone started having a party by jumping around and dancing. The monk was drinking fake shots surrounded by girls, it was a party atmosphere. It was fascinating to watch Crystal, the capuchin monkey, follow every instruction given by its trainer, Tom Gunderson. She was always in front of the camera and she was a bloody good actor! She had worked with some of Hollywood's biggest directors. A tall, crusty, thin hippie with a beard was getting a bit too rowdy. During his moment of fame, he seemed to be trying to take advantage of the camera to steal the spotlight. The hippie abused some people. In no time at all, Allan marched into the bar, grabbed the hippie and flung him out! I loved it. He didn't take any bullshit; we all had a job to do and we didn't need any twats. The sequence was reset and we started to film the fight sequence.

Todd Phillips, the director, called "Action." I was ready and raring to go. I was at the bar with Ron, casually drinking. Bradley came up from behind me and put his arm over my shoulder to order a drink. He spilled his drink and it splashed onto me. I pushed Bradley back into the bar patrons and I said, "Hey, watch it!" Bradley lunged forward and threw a haymaker punch at me, knocking me down to the side of the bar. I broke a few sugar glass bottles as I fell forward. The crowd reacted, screaming. Then the mayhem ensued when I fell to the ground and the entire cast jumped on me, like Chelsea and Millwall fans kicking off on a Saturday! It was crazy, I loved it! The scene was like watching two bulls in a China shop, pushing and shoving and breaking everything in their path. It was chaotic, but in the best way possible. All the cast punched me and kicked me down after I hit the deck. Then, "Cut." Was called.

The crowd in the bar was ecstatic. Shortly after, Bradley and I shook hands and had a quick joke. This was teamwork. Soon after, Allan and Todd Phillips came in and thanked me and Ron. We got the whole sequence in one take. They were very happy. They saved time and money because of our efforts! In addition, I received a nice financial bonus. My gold badge for the day! We had a few still photos taken for the end credits and then I was wrapped! I hung around the set for the remainder of the evening, I watched how they filmed certain scenes. Watching the riot scene with a hundred riot police officers and *The Hangover 2* team was enjoyable. Following the night's shooting, I had to get home sharpish as I had a movie casting the next day. Within a week or so of *The Hangover 2* leaving town, I went back down to the bar to see how the English bar owner was getting on, he was long gone. The bar was closed and refitted and a new name called Dr. BJs. A year later, *The Hangover Part 2* was released. The fight scene was cut short to my disappointment. It could have been due to time constraints or a dropped story thread. I appear briefly in a flashback scene in the film, where Bradley Cooper

It Ain't All Glitz & Glamour

and I get drunk in the bar. Blink and you will miss me! You will see me again in the flashback picture credits when Mike Tyson announces the credits at the end of the film. It was frustrating to be cut from a movie, but it was also a learning experience, as there were plenty more cuts to come!

When I worked on *The Scorpion King*, one of the actors was so happy he had a speaking role. After the film was released, he found out he had been cut. After waiting over 18 months for that scene, he was so deflated. Your career depends on those scenes. During the filming of *The Impossible*, my scene was cut. I worked on that movie for three weeks. I worked on Owen Wilson's *No Escape* for about three weeks too. *No Escape* featured a cool scene where I helped Owen block the gunmen from getting to the roof, but my scene was cut when the movie was released. There are times when the scenes fit and there are times when they don't. This is like working on a jigsaw puzzle. You spend weeks building it, but in the end, the picture may not turn out the way you expected, you have to accept it and move on. The producers own the rights to the footage, they can be brutal and you have no control over this. This is the reality of the film industry, as producers have the final say over what stays in a movie and what doesn't. Even if an actor has worked on the movie for months, they can still be cut without their knowledge. It's an unfortunate reality of the film industry and it's something actors just have to accept.

TAKE 7

November 2011 was a hectic month. After hearing that Nicolas Winding Refn was casting for a gangster film, called *Only God Forgives,* I really wanted to participate. My favourite Viking film was *Valhalla Rising* which he directed and I also liked his other projects *Bleeder, Bronson* and *Drive*. When the casting department put out the casting call, I chose two characters. The first was Yuri, a bodyguard and the second was Dimitri, a mob boss. Two of these characters were running clubs in Bangkok and engaging in all sorts of criminal activity. They were vicious and ruthless individuals who would do anything to get what they wanted. I had a good feeling about the audition and I went in with confidence. I thought this would be right up my alley. The audition would involve lines and a terrible torture scene involving ice picks and tongue cutting. During the first audition, Ron and I assisted each other with the casting. There was no doubt in my mind that I would play one of these characters in this film. In preparation for my casting, I developed a character breakdown. I asked the casting director many questions about this guy's background, personality and other factors. The answers he gave were very basic. My character was a gangster, a club owner and a hitman and he would undergo a horrific torture scene involving ice picks.

I used my past life experiences as the basis for the character I was going to audition for. I modelled my character on a couple of the guys I used to know in my youth. There was quite a bit of violence in the UK in the 1980s, especially in market towns and cities. There were football hooligans and the last of the youth cults. Everyone was up for a ruck. It certainly seemed that way for working-class men. Every weekend, there were fights, especially in pubs, or you heard about something kicking off down the road. In my late teens and early twenties, I hung out with a group of notorious guys. My memories of that time are filled with stupidity and meaninglessness. There was always a fight between this guy and that guy, assaulting this guy and knocking him out. Some served prison sentences for violent crimes such as extortion, robbery and even murder. I witnessed baseball bat fights, brass knuckle duster fights, stabbings, gang fights, torture and all kinds of crazy shit. It was a culture of violence and aggression and many people turned to it to gain respect or a sense of belonging. If we had access to guns, I know for a fact that a few people would have been blown away. Maybe one day I will write a book about those dark times.

Back in the day, if our gang met up in the city on the weekends, there would be some kind of mindless violence. This violence would often take the form of drunken brawls, vandalism, or petty theft. We used to call Saturday nights "Cracking Heads Night." As young, stupid and impressionable as we were, we were all trying to be men!

The Alpha male! Our gang reflected the culture around us, which was full of violence, aggression and competition. We all wanted to show our strength and toughness by engaging in these activities. In the process, we became desensitized and unaware of the consequences. A young, impressionable man has a lot of testosterone running through his veins and testosterone channeled in the wrong direction can be dangerous. We were out on the town one night and it was quiet for a change!

On the way home, we were walking through the city centre, having a drink and a laugh. Jeff, one of our guys, got into a conversation with a guy who was walking through the same area. The two seemed to know each other. Everything was going well and we were waiting for Jeff to finish his conversation, so we could leave. Then it all went pear shaped. There was a heated argument between the two. After some pushing and shoving, this guy pulled out a knife and pointed it at Jeff's face. Since the knife had a red handle and a three-inch blade, I recognised it as a Swiss army knife. Then he used the knife to stab Jeff in the face.

Jeff was stabbed in the lip, cut across the gums and teeth and had his jugular vein pierced. The knifer pulled the knife out of Jeff's neck and threatened us. His mood was manic, he was scared and he was high. There was blood flowing from Jeff's mouth and his face looked like it had a piece of ham hanging from it. A strand of blood gushed from Jeff's neck every few seconds as the beat of his heart increased. He was in shock. The only time Jeff realised what had happened was when he saw blood splattering everywhere. Jeff smiled, but his face showed fear. He looked down, saw the pool of blood near his feet and collapsed to the ground, screaming helplessly. Jeff's screams, echoed through the arcade and the sound was so intense, that people stopped in their tracks. Everyone in the area, was terrified and everyone was in shock. The sight of Jeff's blood-soaked body and the sound of his screams were too much to bear and they were impossible to ignore. We put pressure on the wound, but the blood just kept flowing. His screams were a reminder of the severity of the injury and the helplessness we felt. He passed out on the ground, as more blood splattered from him.

The attacker bolted and me and my friend Bruce, chased the knifer through the streets. Three other members of the gang called 999 and with help from the public, they tried to stem the blood flow. The knifer got away through a Chinese restaurant. Apparently, the police thought we were the ones who had done the dirty deed on Jeff, so they tried to arrest us. That night, Jeff was saved by the emergency services. Somebody was watching over him. As a result of a failed drug deal, Jeff was stabbed in the face. Donald Lyn Frost once said, "Drugs are hell disguised as heaven." That seems about right to me. My friend Bruce was also stabbed in the stomach and arms a few months after this incident over some stupidity. It is tragic that both guys were young and naive at the time. Both are now dead. They both died within a few years of each other. Neither of them had even reached their mid-twenties. The lives of these two people could have been so different. As a villain in films, I now bring my past experiences to life and show the public what happens when you play the game of death.

In my opinion, if any of the scenes in my films turn you off, then that's a positive. When I have to play a role with this kind of excessive violence, I revert back to those dark times and keep it as realistic as possible. This is exactly what I did for *Only God Forgives*. During my audition, I poured all my emotions and life experiences into my character. Eyes, ears and tongue were cut out and ice picks were used to stab me. I recalled my dark times. We auditioned for about 30 minutes, followed by an interview. My gut instinct told me that I had gotten a part, but I couldn't tell which one. I was happy with either of them. I left the casting with confidence that I had smashed it.

My next audition was for a movie called *Sming*. The production approached me after seeing me in *Elephant White*. I was to play a hunter of wild cats. This was a Thai-produced movie and was going to hit all major cinemas in Thailand, so I thought, why not? Playing a hunter would be easy. I would have some English dialogue and get some substantial screen time. The synopsis went like this, Pran Boon, a hunter, saves a child's life by killing a young tiger. However, later, Pran faces the tiger's mother and she takes revenge on him.

The casting was straight-forward enough. They gave me an old rifle, the type you would shoot a moose with and a cool costume. Which consisted of a beige Pith helmet, brown leather knee-high boots and a khaki old-school bush jacket. I needed to pretend I was hunting a tiger and do some dialogue with my hunter friends. I felt like the hunter, Russell Van Pelt, from the original *Jumanji* film. My audition was shot on a green screen. Green screens are key components in film and television production. The green background is replaced with another image, typically a computer-generated one that gives the illusion that the scene is taking place somewhere else. It was fun and I knew I had nailed the casting. Within 30 minutes of leaving the audition, I was confirmed. Things were really picking up for me. Then that afternoon, I attended another casting for a production called *Vikingdom*.

Vikingdom was a Viking movie about a forgotten king, Eirick, who is tasked with impossible odds to defeat Thor, the God of Thunder. They had a massive $15.8 million budget. There was a rumour that it would be the next Gladiator. It was on my bucket list to be in a Viking movie, so I was looking forward to the casting. The auditions for actors in Southeast Asia were held on the roof of a low-budget hotel, of all places, which I found strange. A movie with that kind of budget and they auditioned everyone on a roof top! The casting directors must have put a few quid in their pockets that day, as I don't think it was meant to be cast there. Two very corrupt Malaysian casting directors handled the casting. During the audition process for the film, the casting directors sent one guy to Kuala Lumpur to cast. One of the requirements was that all his body hair had to be shaved off. After going down to KL, they shaved off all of his hair and he was not selected for the role. Cheeky bastards! He was bald as a coot! He must have been so pissed off! To top it off, apparently, he never received his payment when he returned home either. The things people do for a role in a movie never ceases to amaze me! When I went to do my audition on the roof, it started to rain, but they still went ahead with the casting. That's how seriously they were taking it. The Texan loitered on top of the roof and watched everyone audition, but he didn't say much to anyone. He acted as if he were above all the guys in Bangkok. He seemed very close to the two casting directors. I did my audition as best as I could despite the rain and left. I was confirmed for *Vikingdom* a few days later.

I received my filming schedule for *Sming* and *Vikingdom*. I was then faced with a dilemma because my shooting days conflicted. I had to choose whether I wanted to film for *Vikingdom* or for *Sming*. I had to weigh the pros and cons of each and decide which would be the best option for me. *Sming* would be released in Southeast Asia and I would have more lines. *Vikingdom* had a few lines and was going to be released worldwide. For the first time, I had conflicting schedules and I had to decline a film.

It was like being faced with a fork in the road and not knowing which direction to take. I had to carefully consider my options before making a decision and ultimately, I had to choose the one that I thought would benefit my career. I decided to go with *Vikingdom*. When I contacted the producers of *Sming*, I told them I had conflicting days and could not do the role. Due to time constraints, they were unable to fly in any other actor, so they had to substitute me with an obese actor who made Jabba the Hut look small. During that time, I had no idea that this pre-madonna was watching every move I made in the film industry. It turned out that he was one of my biggest trolls, so I must have been doing something right!

A few months later, I was in Malaysia playing a Viking captain called, The Captain of Jomsberg. Filming took place in a massive studio just outside Kuala Lumpa. Now you may think it's strange for a Viking movie to film in that neck of the woods. At first, I thought so too, but they were filming in a huge studio. There were sound stages for Viking halls, Viking castles and Viking ships and it was impressive. With every detail carefully planned and constructed, it was like stepping into a Viking world. As part of my costume, I wore boots, chain mail, a cloak, helmet and had a big sword. The costume made me look cool. Playing these types of roles was where I wanted to be in the film industry.

We shot in a massive Viking Hall, on my first day on set. The attention to detail was remarkable, as the filmmakers used authentic materials and techniques to construct the hall. The stone walls, torches and fireplace all provided a realistic atmosphere that was immersive and captivating. We stood guard, protecting our king, as Eirick (Dominic Purcell) marched in with his men. Within his team was a talented English actor called, Craig Fairbrass. He was playing the character of Sven. I was chuffed and surprised when he walked into the main hall. I had seen Craig in the first *Rise of the Footsoldier* and I thought he did a terrific job. That film inspired me and gave me goosebumps. It was so real. My main aim all along in my acting career was to get into a film like that.

In the Viking Hall, the main cast did their lines and I watched in awe, taking everything in. Yet again, it was an inspiring moment watching the pros at work. I met another great actor during that sequence called Patrick Murray. He played Mickey Pearce in *Only Fools and Horses* and was in one of my favourite movies, *Scum*. Patrick was playing a wizard, I didn't recognise him at first, as he had a big white beard and big eyebrows and he looked like Gandalf from *The Lord of the Rings*. We got along well and he was a very friendly chap. I found him to be very knowledgeable and passionate about the industry. It was a pleasure to meet him and he provided me with a lot of useful advice. The next morning, at breakfast, I told Craig, "Great job on *Rise of the Footsoldier* mate." We hadn't spoken at this point. He was surprised. He didn't seem to know I was English until we started talking. I think he thought I was German or Dutch. There were only five Englishmen on the project out of a cast and crew of a few hundred. Consequently, we bonded well, being hundreds of miles from home in Malaysia. We had breakfast every day together, which helped us become friends and get to know one another.

After a few days, another scene in the Viking Hall was scheduled to shoot. In this scene, I would walk into the king's hall with two other captains and find our king poisoned by the wizard. I went to the wardrobe and got dressed. The props department were making Viking helmets out of rugby balls. They cut them in half, sprayed them with matt silver paint and attached rivets to them. While watching them make these helmets, I got dressed. When they put the chain mail on me, I felt like I was carrying a heavy weight. The chain mail weighed around 60kg. I couldn't work it out, as it seemed to weigh a lot heavier than the one, I had tried on previously, a few days before. After the costume designer placed a metal helmet on my head, I was barely able to move. It weighed seven kilograms and was made of pure steel. My sword and shield were then given to me and I could hardly hold them either. I said to the designer, "This doesn't feel right." He replied in a grumpy tone, "It's your costume, get on with it!" I didn't say anything else, as I didn't want to cause any problems. The only thing was, that l had to walk very slowly to the film set, because the weight of the amour was so heavy. It was like doing an intense workout with weights holding me down. I don't know how the Vikings went into battle with all that amour on. If I got hit, I would fall over from the first blow like a ton of bricks! I gritted my teeth and thought, "OK, it's only a movie, if the Vikings can do it with all this shit on their back, so can I!"

As I made my way to the set, I walked like Talos, the bronze statue in the famous scene from *Jason and the Argonauts.* By the time I got to the Kings Hall, I was knackered. I could hardly lift my head up to look at the king. My fellow Vikings wondered what was wrong with me, as I couldn't turn my head to look at them. I moved around as if I were wearing a neck brace! The problem was trying to balance the bloody heavy helmet on my head so it wouldn't fall off. Every time I moved my head when I spoke, it slid to the side, covering my eyes. It was frustrating. I was determined to make a good impression, but it was difficult considering the circumstances. I looked at the other Viking performers and they walked around with ease. I thought, well, I must be a wimp then. Then I noticed the different colours of chain mail between me and the other Vikings. I was told to go to the starting position for our scene. I was so uncomfortable. I waited and then I could hear there was a problem, I heard some commotion in the background. The costume designer ran up to me and said, "I've given you the wrong costume!" What I have given you is for a guy who is 7 feet tall." It was such a relief to get it off. They replaced the heavy chain mail with a fake rubber one that was much lighter. At this point, the director got pissed off with the costume designer, as it was taking too much time to change me over into the correct costume. He told him to hurry up. All in all, the wardrobe mishap was resolved and I was able to begin the scene without any further delay. But they didn't change my helmet.

I patiently waited for action to be called. After they called it, I walked into the main hall with the two other Viking captains. I had to balance the helmet on my head when walking and I had to keep my posture upright. I had to walk slower than the other Vikings. It was like when you were a kid and you did the bean bag race, with the bean bag on your head, but in my case, it was 7 kg of pure steel. I stopped on my mark and the king sat lifeless on his throne and my helmet fell off my head and fell to the ground. The director asked, "What is wrong now? I replied, "The helmet is too heavy, I can't move and it's too big for my head. He said, "There is no time for a changeover!" Then the wardrobe guy came running to me. They stuffed a bit of cardboard inside my helmet to steady it.

"Action!" Was called, I recited my lines as best as I could under the circumstances. At the same time worrying that the helmet was going to fall off my head. The Viking captain next to me then delivered his lines. He said them in a mixture of

Spanish and English. We were all confused and so was the director. The director said to him, "Try again!" When the Viking captain attempted his lines again, the same thing happened, he spoke in Spanish English and I thought, this guy is in the wrong movie, he should be in a spaghetti western! The director lost his patience and said, "What is this?" The Spanish chap replied in broken English, "Err, these are my lines, sir! The director said, "Give it to Byron." Therefore, I was given his lines. I felt bad for the Spanish guy, but what do you do as we were put on the spot. The director didn't realise this actor was Spanish and couldn't speak English fluently. This surprised me, since I thought the director selected all the actors for the film. The casting agents had pulled a sly one. They had two agendas going on in this movie. They acted as casting directors and talent agents, so they killed two birds with one stone. Recommending their own talent for their own benefit and earning a lucrative commission, both from the production and the actors.

With that heavy helmet on my head, I did my lines and every time I opened my mouth, it shifted to the side of my head covering my eyes. I tried to be as upright as possible to stop it from moving, it was a balancing act. I couldn't deliver the dialogue to the best of my ability because of that stupid helmet, which was disappointing. As I walked away. The helmet fell to the floor and I had a stiff neck. Once I had finished that scene, the wardrobe changed my helmet for the correct one!

I was looking forward to the sequence we would film in the afternoon. There would be enemies of the king entering the hall and threatening us. We would need to draw our swords and defend our king. Our swords were provided by the props department that morning and I thought mine was quite light. I had handled swords previously and they normally weigh around 1.5 kg, but this one was nothing like that. I didn't even bother to take it out of the sheath to look at it. Going back to my position, I didn't think anything more of it. The director called, "Action!" The king's enemies entered the hall and we pulled our swords out to defend the king. When I pulled my sword from the sheaf, I couldn't believe it, there was only half a bloody sword! The Viking next to me did the same thing and only had half a sword too! It was like a *Monty Python* sketch. We all had swords that were cut in half! The director was pissed off and he said, "Cut! What the hell, is this now?"

The props team had made a mistake, which could have cost them time and money. The director had to act quickly and find a solution so that the scene could be filmed the way it was meant to be. Ultimately, it was decided that only some of the Vikings with full swords would be able to draw their swords completely, while others like me would have to fake the shot and draw them halfway. I learned later that the props team had a communication problem that day. They had taken the wrong swords to film at another location with the second unit. We managed to finish the scene over the next few days and my next sequence was going to be shot in a stone quarry a few days later.

On the first day we filmed at the quarry, I saw the Texan in the make-up tent. Despite sitting directly next to me, the

Texan did not even look at me or speak to me. It was like he had blinkers on. When I said "Hi!" He blatantly ignored me. He was like a child, sulking. I was baffled so I tried to get a response from him, I said "How is it going?" He still did not respond. He then got up out of his make-up chair and walked off. This guy was 56 at the time a fully grown man and lost in his own bullshit in his head, which I found sad. We had given him lots of opportunities for film jobs, which he begged for and we recommended him to dozens of people. We had lent him money, which he never returned, so I struggled to figure out what was going on in his head. We had helped this guy so many times and in the end, he didn't even have the common courtesy to even thank us. Maybe he thought he was better than us?

I spoke with a stunt horseback rider on set one afternoon and he knew the Texan. I said to him, "What's up with the Texan? He's not speaking to me?" The horse rider replied smiling, "The Texan doesn't want to speak to anyone below him in the cast! Looks like you're below him!" I replied, "Is that right!" I thought it was so childish. This moment seemed to be the turning point for the Texan in his life. Hollywood was calling! The horse rider continued, "The Texan said that Ron and I were paying casting directors for roles, that's why we were getting so much work!" I laughed when I heard this. The Texan was deluded. Maybe the narcotics he was taking had twisted his mind. After all the things we had done for him, he repaid us like that.

As we were shooting in the sun for the stone quarry scene, they were cheating the shot for wintertime. The quarry was the perfect place to film, as the rocks provided the appropriate background and the terrain was just right for what they wanted to achieve. The filmmakers had to create an artificial winter environment by adding snow and other effects to the footage later in post-production. They used CGI and special effects to make the snow fall, as well as to create the illusion of a cold winter day. It was a funny day that day, as one of the actors I knew quite well actually lied and said that he could ride a horse. It was essential for his character in the film to ride. He didn't have a clue how to ride a horse and was unsafe, but the production couldn't change the scene. So, they stuck him on an old diesel barrel with a saddle on it and filmed him like that!

It was the first time I had a stunt double in my acting career. The production asked me if I would mind having a stunt double, since I would still be credited and paid, so I said no problem! After getting my face rubbed in the dirt for a few years, it was nice to have somebody else to do my stunts for me. It was just a matter of getting on and off a horse and participating in a battle scene. I showed my face from various angles and then that was it. I filmed a small scene with Dominic Purcell and then I was wrapped. Oh, and I didn't die in this movie. I was on *Vikingdom* for about four weeks and most of it was hanging around to be honest with you. It was a good experience and I met some good people on the set. I kept in touch with Craig. I was now looking forward to an exciting project with an inspiring director who would cause uproar at the Cannes Film Festival. Upon returning to Bangkok, I had lunch with the *Drive'* director, Nicolas Winding Refn. For me, that was a big moment. He basically quizzed me about my past and some of the guys I hung around with back in the day. His fascination with violence was obvious. I told him many stories, including the incident with Jeff and many other encounters. I suspected he also wanted to know about my past experiences so he could better assess my suitability for the role. I told him that I put what I had experienced in my past and incorporated that into my character when I did the casting. According to him, I was the only one who came to the casting and did the audition differently.

He said, "There were several male actors casting for the role, but they all acted the same way." He likely saw something unique in my casting that made him see me as the most suitable person for the character. At this point in my career, I tried to be as natural as possible in all my castings. As I recall all those actors I had spoken with, they all advised me to just be myself and put the character in my heart! I left the meeting knowing I had hit the mark, but I still didn't know which role I had landed. While waiting for the casting department to reply, I continued to work on films and TV commercials. I had come to the point when I was invited to an audition, I would show up, do it and then forget about it. I wouldn't dwell on things. It was like playing a game of roulette, where I knew that no matter what the outcome, I would eventually be OK. I just had to accept whatever happened and move on to the next opportunity. The film business is a numbers game. This strategy allowed me to remain resilient and focus on growing my career, regardless of the outcome. I received a reply a few weeks later. It read, "Hi Byron, I am happy to let you know that Nicolas has selected you for Yuri, the mafia boss! For now, the roles of Dimitri and Yuri have been combined into one character, but this may change either way. The scene is in Yuri's gay bar in Silom. There goes your reputation!" My optimism was high at this point, as I knew I could greatly benefit from this film. I knew that being part of such a high-profile film, would be a great way to increase my visibility and build my acting career. I was also excited to work with such accomplished actors as Ryan Gosling and Kristin Scott Thomas. It was time to pull my socks up and try even harder.

When I began preparing for *Only God Forgives*, a prosthetic head and a fake tongue had to be made for me. In my torture scene, my eyes were going to be cut out, so they made five prosthetic heads, so they could use a scalpel blade to cut into my eyelids. Also, my tongue was going to be pulled out with some pinchers and then cut off. The prosthetic head was made to be an exact replica of the size and shape of my head and the eyelids were made to be very thin and flexible, so the blade could cut them easily. The prosthetic head also had to have a realistic texture, so it could blend in with my own skin. I found that to be quite an interesting experience. My prosthetics were made at a place called QFX in Bangkok.

I found the place to be truly fascinating. It was a place where people's heads, dinosaurs, zombies and torsos of bodies were created. They had made prosthetics for many Hollywood films. I found it incredible that they were able to create such realistic-looking prosthetics and I was amazed by the amount of attention to detail and craftsmanship that went into each piece. When I walked around the studio, I saw only one male person there, the owner of QFX and all his other employees were women. I asked him, "Why is there only women working here? He replied, "They absolutely love this kind of work. It's not a job that many men want to do!"

This is how my face was cast. A rich moisturising cream was applied to my face. To breathe, straws were placed in my nose. My face was then covered in putty. It was alginate, a powder made from seaweed that becomes a paste when mixed with water. Dentists also use it to take impressions of teeth. A cast was created after the putty was placed on my face. The experience would be unbearable if you were suffering from claustrophobia. As a result, my face was completely covered and I was unable to move. To cast my eyelids, I had to keep my eyes closed. The experience was like wearing a thick rubber mask over your head and being unable to see anything. It was like a sensory prison, with the only movement allowed being my own breathing. After the alginate had dried, I had a negative mould on my face. An exact replica of my face was created using silicone rubber, which was then cast in plaster. It was an interesting experience. As soon, as I had my face done, it was time for my tongue to be cast. The putty was placed on a plate and put inside my mouth, just like when they make dentures. I bit into it and then the artists went to work on my fake tongue too.

When I got home, I received an email telling me my character was named Byron. Seems like the directors liked that name! I started a breakdown of my character. I knew he was a ruthless club owner and could organise hits. So with this in mind, I took something from my past. I've known some pretty crazy guys in my time. Among the guys I've known who have been in trouble with the law, most of them have been victims of circumstance. They started off doing petty crime, then one thing led to another and then they fell into the criminal world. As a result of my naiveté and stupidity when I was young, I got a criminal record. It was then that I should have learned my lesson. It didn't take long for things to spiral out of control for me. This came to a head when a police car was stolen and I nearly got sent down with my fellow comrades. It is important to understand that most criminals believe they are doing the right thing. They can justify their actions by believing that they are not criminals, ignoring the consequences of their actions. There is an us versus them mentality among them. This is exactly what I put into my character. My goal was to be on point with this movie because the lead actors were world-class award-winning actors. Preparations for my scenes began. The one thing I did was to avoid all contact with Vithaya Pansringarm, who played the police officer Chang, who cut my eyes out in the film. I punched the punch bag every single day with a picture of his face on it. I didn't mean any harm to the man whatsoever, as we are friends and he's such a great guy. This was my way of method acting. By using this technique, I was able to channel my anger and frustration into something productive. As a result, I was able to focus on the character I was portraying and get into the right mindset for the scene by creating a physical manifestation of my enemy. I did this for three months before we were due to film. Several days before we were supposed to shoot, the script was changed and some of my and other actor's scenes were cut. It was disappointing, but I thought, well, I'm still in the film, so I'll make the most of it.

I met Ryan Gosling on a few of the sets. He was playing the character of Julien. I offered to teach him Muay Thai. As we talked one night, he asked, "How long have you spent in prison, Byron?" As I giggled, I replied, "I have yet to embark on an adventure in the slammer." He reciprocated my smile and I couldn't tell if he truly believed me or not. Perhaps he assumed I was avoiding the topic. At least he acknowledged that I appeared to fit in, making it somewhat of a compliment.

The day had come to begin filming with Kristin Scott Thomas. Her character in the film was called, Crystal, Julien's mother. The scene was shot at a bar in a red-light district. I found the bar to be strange. The interior was dark and there was a stage and church pews. It was a gay bar, with a religious theme. Trust me, you wouldn't want to attend Sunday school there. However, it was the perfect location to shoot a movie. I could smell a terrible stench of sexuality in the place. I was told during shows, punters would get up to all kinds of tricks down the aisles, including masturbating. There was no way I was touching anything in that bar. Overall, it was a night that I will never forget.

When it came time to film our scene, Crystal and I sat down on the church pews. Nicolas didn't like the filming angle, so then we went to shoot the scene at the bar. We reset ourselves and that's when I watched a debauched thing happen. Despite being pretty messed up; it was part of the

It Ain't All Glitz & Glamour

script. A theatrical lady-boy and a lady proudly walked on the stage. They were both wearing silk robes. They casually took off the robes and then engaged in doggy-style sex on stage. As the lady-boy thrust away, the lady smiled as they simulated sex. Maybe they were trying to win an Oscar, as they seemed to love the moment. They looked like evil, smiling Manikin dolls. As I watched the live sex act, I tried to maintain a straight face. The director wanted me to be mesmerized by the sex scene, while Crystal talked to me in disgust. It was mad. I was filming a scene with an award-winning actress known by millions and watching a live sex act only a few metres away.

At one point, I nearly laughed as they were both very hairy in the privates. The never regions were styled like something from the 1970's. It was like they had thick afro-tumbleweed pubic hair in the crotch department. I always remember, Nicolas telling me to relax my face and to be as natural as possible during the takes, which was quite hard at times. With the show going on. Around 22 takes later, we were finally finished with that scene. I had seen enough sex that night to last me a lifetime. The sex performers on the stage proudly bowed to us after they had finished their scene as if they were cabaret performers in the West End.

As you can imagine, it was a long night. In my career, I have never experienced footage being shot in as many takes as Nicolas did. However, I do understand his work logic and he has so far been the best director, I have ever worked under. The guy is a true master. The sexual scene did not make it into the movie. It even shocked me. Since it wasn't a typical movie scene, this scene could have been considered controversial. It may have been seen as too explicit and inappropriate for certain audiences, so it could have been deemed unsuitable for the film when it made its way into the final edits.

A few days later, my major torture scene was about to begin. This scene was going to be so real and gory. I wanted it to be second to none. I really wanted to make a strong impression on the viewer. It was a turning point in my acting career and I didn't want to waste it. I was determined to make sure that this scene was as intense and believable as possible. I knew that I had to really put my emotions into it to capture the audience's attention. I was prepared to give everything I had to it, no matter the cost. It was shot in another gay bar. Inside the bar there were neon lights, lots of flowers, paintings of naked bodies and statues of naked people. It was like walking into another world, one totally different from the reality outside. It was a world of fantasy and exploration, a world where anything was possible. The atmosphere was surreal, with the girls wearing colourful dresses, seated around the room and the lights creating a magical atmosphere. It was like being in a fairytale, with the girls as characters from *Alice in Wonderland.*

I took my seat. Nicolas asked me, "What would you do in such a situation, for real?" I replied, "If I knew I was going to die, I would either go for a gun or at least put up a fight since you're going to die anyway. I would go out in a blaze of glory." Nicolas plans, however, were different. The cameras were ready to go, we went for a take. Just before we started the first shot of the night, Nicolas said to me, "Byron, this is your house and nobody comes into your house and tells you what to do! He called, "Action!" I turned to my dark thoughts and knew that at this point, the filth was entering my domain. A police officer called Kim walked over to me, as I sat watching a lady sing on my stage. I got up to confront Kim and he front kicked me back down into my chair. He pointed his revolver at me. My mind regressed to the days of my youth, hanging around with all those nutters. I filled my heart with hatred. I thought back to my father abusing my mother. I was method acting, putting all those negative times in my soul and projecting them into my character. Kim stood in front of me and I wanted to kill him. The atmosphere was tense. The lady stopped singing.

As Kim stared at me with contempt, pointing the gun at me, he knew it was time for me to meet the devil. With disrespect, I looked at him. How dare he point a gun at me and enter my house? I was fearless, I was a god! During my youth, there was an incident that stuck with me and this scene reminded me of it. This is what I put into my soul. I said to Kim, "Who the fuck are you? Get out of my club." I kept staring at him with hate in my eyes while he pointed his revolver at me. Kim said, "Remember, ladies, whatever happens, close your eyes. And you men, take a good look." I replied with venom in my tone. "Can somebody tell me what the fuck this cunt is trying to say?" Kim answered back, "Who put out the hit?" I replied, "Go fuck yourself, how about that?" Kim carried on pointing the gun at me, then the director called "Cut." We did this for approximately 20 takes. I was sweating with emotion. They had to come and wipe me down in-between scenes. I was exhausted after all those takes when

Nicolas finally said, "Let's move onto the torture scene. The scene was reset. I was restrained in both arms and legs. Some clamps were made to sit under my arms and thighs. There was no way I could move. The chair was too heavy for me to topple over. I would be clamped in that chair for up to 12 hours. The cameras were ready to go and we went for a take.

As Chang walked around my bar, all the girls had their eyes closed. He walked over to an ice bucket filled with bottles of champagne. Taking out two ice picks, he slowly approached me like a predator. There was no escaping this guy, he was a god. I felt powerless and helpless, as I watched Chang move closer. I knew that I had no chance against him. I was filled with dread as I realised, that I had no choice but to face him and accept my fate. Chang stood in front of me. After pulling up the ice picks in the air, he thrust them down into my arms, pinning me to the chair. I screamed in pain. My gaze was fixed on Chang as he leered down at me. In my mind's eye, I saw Jeff lying there in a pool of blood and screaming his heart out. In my heart, I felt fear as I screamed so loudly. Jeff's scream was my scream. Chang said. "Why?" I replied. "She said you murdered her son. She wanted you dead." Then the director called, "Cut!" A filmmaking masterclass was taking place and I was in my element. By the tenth take, I was losing my voice and needed a honey drink to lubricate my throat. This experience showed me that Nicolas had a deep appreciation for how to capture emotion in his films. He understands that it requires multiple takes, to capture a flawless scene and is willing to do whatever it takes to get it. I was exhausted and drained and this was the emotion he wanted to portray. I had to repeat this over 22 times and have the same emotion during each take. Finally, we nailed it. During the short break between scenes, a few girls complained about the screaming. It seemed like I was giving them nightmares. As a result, the production gave them ear plugs.

The cinematographer's wife and children watched the shoot. Although his kids thought it was fine, his wife thought it was a bit too much! Everyone was being put through a live horror show. During the filming, Larry Smith, the cinematographer, questioned the logic. He said this to Nicolas. "Look, this guy would probably die of fear or shock, once you put those things through his thighs and hands. He'd be dead by the time you reached his ears. But hey, it's a movie, so you can do what you want!" He went on to say in one interview, "It was quite harrowing to shoot this scene."

After the break, I went back to sit in my chair and prepare for my demise. The props department came over and they screwed in the ice picks into the clamps they had made to keep me in place. I looked like a human pin cushion, as the ice picks were stuck in my arms and thighs. I was ready to roll. "Action" was called. Chang walked around the bar. He regarded me as scum. He picked out a fruit knife from the fruit bowl.

The phantom menace approached me. As my death loomed, I was unable to move. He put me in a headlock. I could feel my heart pounding in my chest as he slowly pulled the knife above my head in an act of terror that overwhelmed me. Tears filled my eyes. Blood from the cuts flowed down my face. He spoke to me like a god, judging his children. It was like a scene from *The Three Wise Monkeys*. See no evil, hear no evil and speak no evil. Chang said. "You cannot see what's good for you. Better you cannot see." The fruit knife was used to cut into my eyelids. As I shouted in pain, I thought back to the days watching my father hit my mother. I saw her in pain. I also remembered Jeff's screams. I remembered a guy who I witnessed being tortured when he was handcuffed to a toilet, having the living daylights kicked out of him and was screaming for mercy. I screamed and screamed and screamed!

As Chang walked away, I was nearly dead. After picking out an ice pick from the fruit bowl, Chang returned. He said, "You have an opportunity here, but you are stubborn. You do not want to listen. If you do not want to hear, then stop listening." I was stabbed in the ear with the ice pick, bursting my eardrums and piercing my brain. The screaming continued until I was completely exhausted. After another 20 or so takes, my scene was complete. "Cut!" Was finally called.

There was silence for a moment. I think I gave some of them nightmares. They must have been relieved when it was over. The production team and the director unstrapped me from the chair. Then they congratulated me. I had lost my voice and my throat was raw. After the sequence was finished, some of the ladies were still sitting in their positions. As a result, the production team had to walk around to see what was wrong. They had bloody fallen asleep! Some of them fell asleep despite the screaming, because they had pushed the earplugs, so far into their ears. It was a funny moment and it was a good way to end the evening. I think Nicolas cut the tongue scene because he was satisfied with what he captured that night.

I'm sure you're wondering how they did this torture scene with the ice picks and knives. The knife was a prop knife that looked just like the real thing. The blade was made of soft rubber. A cartridge of blood was also inside the knife, so when the knife cut into my eyelids, blood flowed down my face. The ice pick retracted as he drove it into my flesh, creating the illusion that it was going in. That's movie magic at its best. Several days later, my prosthetic head was used for the close-up shots. There were blood packs in the eye sockets of my fake head. Which were sealed with pipes behind them. A pump filled with blood was connected to the pipes. As a result, blood gushed out when they cut into my eyelids for the close-up shots. The close-up shot was then inserted into the film.

At the end of the shoot, I received a prosthetic head as a trophy. *Only God Forgives*, was released at the 2013 Cannes Film Festival. It was selected to compete for the Palme d'Or, the highest prize at the festival. As well as its misogynistic themes, the movie received criticism for its violent and sexual portrayals. A lot of people in the audience that night walked out in disgust, saying the ice pick torture scene was too much. I upset the crowd when they sat there in their tuxes, sipping champagne. It was a great feeling. By injecting a bit of reality into their otherwise idyllic evening, I showed them that violence is far from glamorous. There is nothing nice about violence, even though mankind seems fascinated by it.

Due to conflicting schedules with another movie, I was unable to attend Cannes. My friend Sebastien from *Largo Winch* 2 was doing the security at the festival, he sent me a message saying the audience was left in total shock and his ears were ringing for days from my screaming. I was celebrating this by getting a tattoo done at the time, when a British Channel 5, TV show called Brits in Bangkok, filmed me and Leigh. In essence, they arrived with the intention of creating a visual record of the expat community in Thailand. Their aim was to feature my acting endeavours and Leigh's flourishing dance enterprise in a few episodes. Leigh and I agreed to participate, unaware that the result would be a mockery of our efforts. The narrative structure was nonsensical and we were portrayed as foolish, despite contributing our time and talents gratuitously for free. Our agent had cautioned us against getting involved, but we chose to give the creators the benefit of the doubt. However, in hindsight, we deeply regretted our decision. They made a documentary that was basically untrue and a piss take.

Despite these twats doing the dirty on us a few weeks later, I won an award for my *Only God Forgives* torture scene. Mel Gibson's *Braveheart*, disembowelment scene came in at number ten, my scene was ranked at number nine for Watch Mojo's best torture scenes. That's not bad for a geezer from my neck of the woods! I had to laugh at some of the reviews from the newspapers and magazines. The internet was even funnier. Here are some of the comments,

"This is just the start. One scene in this blood-drenched revenge saga sees a man tortured in the most squirm-inducing scene since Reservoir Dogs."

"It is a shockingly violent film; the torture scene is virtually unwatchable. Truly disturbing."

"This, to me, is one of the most fascinating and beautifully done torture scenes in any film I have seen!"

"I've never heard the words beautiful or fascinating used when describing torture before. But ok, whatever. Better not look in your basement, I guess."

"Only people with zero mirror neurons and a highly

superficial appreciation of art like this film!"

Following the worldwide release of *Only God Forgives*, I was fortunate enough to secure an agent in London, marking a pivotal moment in my career, as casting directors began to take notice of me. This experience shaped me in a significant way, as I yearned for fresh, exciting challenges and sought out more prominent acting roles. The film garnered considerable attention and notoriety, causing discussions and conversations to revolve around my name. Unfortunately, along with the support came some trolls, who took to following my every move. However, I saw this as a testament to my success, knowing that I must have been doing something right. One particular individual, a sugar-coated blob by the name of Jabba, took it upon himself to send me emails claiming that the role should have been his. In my eyes, he was nothing but a sore loser. In a bizarre turn of events, he challenged me to a Shakespearean knowledge competition. I must admit, I am not a Shakespearean actor and wouldn't know where to begin. He must have thought he was the master of acting in Bangkok, but I dismissed him as nothing more than a loser seeking attention. Needless to say, I had no time for such foolishness.

My London agent took advantage of my increased visibility in the industry. As a result, I was cast in more roles and received more attention. While casting in London, I caught the eye of a well-known casting director. After the audition, I left and didn't think about it again. My agent called me a few minutes after I arrived home to tell me I had been cast in *Game of Thrones*. It was a pleasant surprise for me. There would be some dialogue in the scene and the scene would be filmed in Malta. However, there is always a catch to anything in life and my character would appear in a full-frontal naked scene. Therefore, you would see my meat and two vegetables! Despite the fact that it would have been a perfect opportunity for me, I declined the offer. I was honoured that they picked me. I wouldn't have had a problem if they wanted to see my backside. I still have no regrets. I'm okay with all kinds of crazy stuff, but nakedness is where I draw the line. I leave it to the pros, like Rocco Siffredi!

My appearance in *Only God Forgives* led to many other roles. It's still the case nowadays, as many casting directors remember me. I am grateful for the opportunity to have worked on that film. My agent advised me to focus more on acting than action. After playing a Russian mafia boss in Goa, I was cast in a BBC television series as a criminal in jail. A German movie required me to play a rough diamond character in a challenging role. In addition to being an ex-army soldier, he was also a mechanic. My mindset was changing at this point, since I was open to more varied roles rather than playing the bad guy. The 100 page script was in German, I had to memorise the words and reply in English. In the final cut, they dubbed over my voice. In spite of my inability to understand what was being said in German, I remained professional and followed the director's instructions. I felt like I was playing a game of charades. While I understood the themes of the movie, I had to act out several parts of the story without understanding the language. I just had to trust my acting skills to convey the story. I stayed in a top hotel for one month in Krabi Thailand, which has some of the finest beaches in the world and received a handsome paycheck. German television aired the film on Live Aid Day. Talk about faking it till you make it.

Afterwards, I did my first horror movie, in which I had my eyes cut out and then fed to me as part of a torture scene. I worked on fight films, TV series and even dramas. The British gangster films were my dream, but I had to keep pushing myself to get in. Still, I had to take the good projects with the bad. Overall, I had to work hard and take risks to pursue my goals. My dream to travel and see the world came true as I travelled to China and all over Asia. My business plan was proving to be successful. I was thriving in the industry! I worked on films with greats such as Christopher Mintz-Plasse, Michael Mando, Hayden Christensen and Nicolas Cage. Whether it be indie productions or high-budget Hollywood flicks, I was absorbing valuable lessons from the cream of the crop and rejecting no offers, no matter how big the role. I saw a change in the industry during this time. Back in the day, it took six months to shoot a movie. As technology has advanced, so have filmmaking techniques. Cameras have gotten smaller and more powerful, allowing for faster shooting. Editing software has also improved, allowing filmmakers to manipulate scenes more easily. Budgets have also shrunk due to illegal downloads. The ability to complete a film quickly is crucial for filmmakers. This is why so many movies now take less than a month to shoot. In the past, I worked on between four and five movies per year. Depending on the role, some actors may have four weeks for their main role. If it's a day player, they may only have one day. After that, you need to look again for the next gig, your nose is constantly on the grindstone. Most people outside the industry believe that once you get a big role, you're a success and can live like a king forever. However, this isn't true, you must work until you can find a job that can support you. It is for this reason that so many actors today try to get roles in television shows. A thousand pounds or twenty grand for a role is not enough to keep you afloat when you only work once a year. There are many actors who live on the breadline. It's only the big stars who make the most money. At the end of the day, the remaining cast members are self-employed contractors who are called in when needed.

It Ain't All Glitz & Glamour

TAKE 8

Not all filmmakers have the luxury of massive budgets to bring their visions to life. While major studios like Warner Bros and Disney have ample resources at their disposal, many exceptional films have been crafted on a shoestring budget. There is a massive worldwide community of independent filmmakers who make movies and have to raise the budgets themselves, or through private investors. It's a huge risk to undertake and is time-consuming. If the film doesn't sell well, you can lose a lot of money. But if the film sells well, it can put you on the map as a major filmmaker. Now I am going to tell you about a film we shot and we had a huge obstacle to overcome while shooting in a country in Asia.

I will never forget that night when I saw tanks take over the streets. During this time, a good friend of mine was filming a feature film and I had been selected as one of the main characters. The producer's name was Bob. We were passionate about what we were doing and not even the military was going to stop us! It's amazing what you can do once you put your mind to it. Now the problem was that Bob had no more

It Ain't All Glitz & Glamour

budget to finish his film. He had a deadline to meet with the distribution and was under pressure to complete it, otherwise the whole project would go pear-shaped. To do well in this industry, you have to take the rough with the smooth and persevere, no matter what, if you want to succeed. Soldiers were on the streets and there was a very tense atmosphere in the city. Bob was desperately trying to figure out how he was going to finish his film, with no funds and to make matters worse there was a state of emergency. One of the biggest dilemmas was that Bob needed a hospital scene to complete the project and this would cost a lot of money which he didn't have. Another obstacle was that the whole of the country was under martial law. So, this was a massive problem to add to the equation. But as the old saying goes, where there's a will, there's a way!

We managed to pull it off, with a very cunning plan. We came up with the idea that we should guerilla shoot in a working hospital. This was going to be an extremely complicated operation, filming in a hospital with martial law in place. It would take a lot of balls to pull that off. We only needed three shots, to complete the movie. Bob then would be home and dry, so we said sod it, let's do it! We thought back to *Only Fools and Horses* when Del Boy once said, "He who dares wins." So like idiots we went for it, with not a care in the world! The first sequence we needed was a shot of my character dressed as a doctor, getting in a lift and walking through some wards. We worked out a basic plan for how we were going to film the scene, we just needed to find a hospital!

So instead of picking a small hospital, we boldly picked the biggest hospital in the city centre! It was the nearest one to us at the time and for some reason, in our crazy minds, it made sense to film there. We carefully scouted the location first from the outside and then went into the building. We casually walked in and made our way to the 10th floor. We thought for some reason, it wouldn't be so busy. I don't know why we thought that, but lucky for us, it wasn't. Good instincts, perhaps? We scouted the floor; it was perfect and we quickly worked out what shots we needed while keeping a straight face and politely smiling at any staff who passed by. The ward had many beds, a reception area, two access lift points, one as you entered the ward and one at the end of the ward to exit. This was perfect for a quick escape. The ward was approximately 30 metres long, so all I needed to do was walk through the ward looking like a doctor and escape down the exit lift pronto, never to be seen again. Job done! The plan was as simple as that. It would only take a few minutes to film if we got it right!

While we were discussing the camera angles in the corridor, there was a nurse at reception who was staring at us. I think she thought we were lost. She pointed to the exit lift and we smiled at her, we walked on and we got in the lift. We made our way down to the ninth floor, got out and waited beside the lift entrance. Bob gave me a white doctor's jacket to put on while he got himself ready to operate the camera. By now, we had another two guys with us. One I will call Dutch, the other Stan. Dutch was the lookout man and he soon gave us the all-clear to start filming.

It Ain't All Glitz & Glamour

We pressed the lift button and the lift promptly arrived with no one in it. I entered the lift still fumbling around, trying to put my white doctor's jacket on, feeling very uneasy about the whole thing and wondering what the hell I was doing. Bob followed me with the camera in hand, Dutch and Stan following close behind, keeping a lookout. Then, just as the lift doors were closing, I couldn't believe my luck, a real doctor got in! At this moment, I thought shit, our cover was blown and I was going to get nicked for impersonating a doctor during a bloody military coup! However, lucky for us, the doctor was so busy with his phone that he didn't take any notice of me in the doctor's jacket He didn't even look up at the cameraman standing beside him. The power of the phone! It was unbelievable, we were very lucky! We only had one floor to go up, as soon as the doors opened, the doctor made his way out and marched off down the hallway, still glued to his phone. As he walked away, we could see he was playing a game. Thank God for Candy Crush Saga!

I waited and watched until he was out of sight, then I casually walked out of the lift. Bob gave me the nod and started to film; it was time for action! I started walking through the ward, looking for the character I was going to rescue, with Bob following me on camera and Dutch and Stan keeping an eye out for security. Now, the funny thing was that the nurse at reception, who saw us earlier, was totally confused that we were back. She couldn't work out what we were doing, judging by the expression on her face, but she didn't confront us. We walked past her, smiled and made our way through the wards. My heart was beating so strong, I just wanted to get out of there. As we were about to exit the ward, I looked back at the nurse and at this point, she was on the phone calling security. I made my way through the ward even quicker, with Bob following and filming me. Dutch was looking hesitant and some of the patients were looking up at us, wondering who the hell we were. At this point, our cover had been blown. We ran to the lift, I pressed the button for the 8th floor, we scrambled in, the doors closed and we got the hell out of there.

We went down to the 8th floor. Now, we thought that if security were coming after us, they would either go to the 10th floor, or wait for us at the ground-floor lift entrance. If we got caught, they would either escort us off the hospital grounds or wait for the army to arrest us. So, we waited on the 8th floor for around 5 minutes out of sight. Just to gauge the situation, I gave Bob back my white doctor's jacket, put a baseball cap on and changed my top. Bob hid the camera and took out the memory card in case we got stopped. We managed to get out of the hospital unchallenged by any security. We casually walked out of the hospital entrance, as we passed a tank and soldiers in the car parking area. We smiled at the soldiers and they smiled back. We made our way to a coffee shop and we went through the footage. It was perfect, we got what we needed. Job Done. What a thrill! Only two scenes were needed now to finish the movie! Now onto the next scene we had to film. We needed a shot of the character I was going to free in the film. This character was played by Bob. We needed a shot of Bob on a bed having tests done, as in the film he was the hostage. The only thing was that we didn't have a hospital bed to film on.

It Ain't All Glitz & Glamour

We discussed the problem and solved it like Einstein within 30 minutes over a cappuccino. We came up with the bright idea to shoot at a dentist. We made our way down a main tourist road, full of high-end shops, malls and much more. We managed to find one, in a high-end shopping centre. It wasn't busy and we boldly walked into the reception and asked if we could speak to the boss. The receptionist called in her boss and we politely asked if we could film in his surgery. Now the dentist asked what the video was going to be used for. We boldly told him it was a happy birthday YouTube clip and that the video was intended as a joke for one of our fathers. Who used to be a dentist and that it would take no more than 5 minutes. We couldn't believe our luck when the dentist obliged. We quickly got our cameras out, then Bob got on the dentist chair and then I put on my white doctor's coat. Dutch started filming a close-up shot of Bob asleep on the chair, it worked a treat. As we were finishing the scene, the dentist walked in and watched us and we all said happy birthday to the camera! We had just pulled off our second guerilla filming stint and we were getting good at it. We thanked the dentist for letting us use his surgery, we made our way out, laughing all the way to the next location, which was going to be even dodgier!

The final shooting location was in the city's heart. We sought to film at a major hospital situated in this area. As we approached the hospital, we noticed military checkpoints along the road, a stark reminder of the ongoing political unrest. Soldiers patrolled the streets, their presence evident as we navigated the neighbourhood. Amidst this tense atmosphere, we reached the hospital entrance, where a group of soldiers stood guard, their machine guns positioned behind a fortification of sandbags and barbed wire. Surprisingly, they didn't question our presence or our destination, instead, they greeted us with smiles, allowing us to pass without incident. This encounter left us with a sense of bewilderment, wondering if they mistook us for tourists or visitors to the hospital. Regardless of their assumption, we proceeded towards the hospital, eager to fulfil our filming obligations. We discovered a side entrance area where stretcher beds were neatly stored. The area was deserted, devoid of any hustle and bustle.

We ventured inside and conducted a quick reconnaissance to assess its suitability for filming. A check-in desk was at the entrance, with a nurse diligently engrossed in paperwork. In a corner lay a bundle of stretchers and wheelchairs, while a long hallway beckoned us towards the main hospital. We made our way through the deserted side entrance, passing by a corner stacked with stretchers and wheelchairs. A long hallway lay before us, leading towards the main hospital. We headed to the hospital canteen, situated opposite the entrance, to finalise our shoot plan. The plan was simple. Bob would play the role of the prisoner, lying lifelessly on a stretcher, while I, clad in the doctor's jacket graciously, would quickly push him through the hospital wards. Dutch would capture the entire scene on camera. With the plan in place, a sense of anticipation filled the air. I eagerly donned the doctor's jacket, ready to reprise my role as the dodgy doctor. The stage was set for an intriguing filming session. We emerged from the canteen and headed back into the storage area. After receiving the green light from Dutch, we sprang into action. Bob hopped onto the nearest stretcher and assumed a lifeless pose, while I swiftly grabbed the handles and began propelling him through the hospital wards like a man possessed. Dutch, our cameraman, trailed us closely, capturing every moment on film. Stan, ever vigilant, kept a watchful eye out for any potential trouble. As we navigated through the bustling ward, a nurse looked up, her face etched with confusion. Her face said it all, "Who the hell are these crazy foreigners?"

Dutch offered her a reassuring smile and a nod, as I continued pushing the stretcher, bulldozing my way through the plastic curtains. The hallway eventually opened into a larger room teeming with people, doctors, nurses, patients and security guards. Our presence had not gone unnoticed. All eyes were on us! Doctors eyed us suspiciously, the security guards pointed in our direction, their faces grim. Realising that our cover was blown, I executed a swift U-turn and made a hasty retreat. With Bob clinging tightly to the stretcher, I propelled us down the hallway at full speed, laughing with fear. The nurse at the reception desk watched in disbelief, as we barged past her again. Plastic curtains were flapping wildly in our wake. Dutch urged us to do a runner. Bob, springing back to life, leaped off the stretcher and joined me in our mad dash for freedom. As we fled, I hastily removed my doctor's jacket and chucked it in a bin. While Dutch and Stan raced alongside us, their breaths echoing through the sterile corridors. As we were dodging and weaving through the maze of vehicles navigating the hospital grounds, we kept a constant vigil over our shoulders. Our hearts were pounding in anticipation. We finally managed to lose the security.

A taxi driver, having just dropped off a patient, opportunely cruised past us. Dutch, with his trademark resourcefulness, hailed down the cab just in the nick of time. Piling into the taxi, we instructed the driver to whisk us away. As we approached the hospital gates, a wave of apprehension washed over us. Soldiers were meticulously inspecting every passing vehicle. We braced ourselves for the inevitable confrontation and our minds were racing with potential escape routes. To our astonishment, the soldiers merely glanced at our taxi, their eyes widening as they recognised occupants of foreign descent. With a reassuring smile and a friendly wave, they gestured us through the gates, allowing us to slip away into the bustling city.

Bob had successfully accomplished to finish his film. Some of the footage we captured made it into the final cut. Currently engrossed in his third cinematic masterpiece, Bob is poised to cement his position as a visionary director and producer. His passion, expertise, exceptional visual storytelling skills have inspired me to embark on my own filmmaking journey. I salute you, Bob! Your unwavering determination and unwavering belief in your craft have ignited my passion for filmmaking. In hindsight, if you asked me would I ever do this again, my answer would be a resounding "No." I later discovered that impersonating a doctor carries a hefty penalty, potentially extending to three years of imprisonment.

It Ain't All Glitz & Glamour

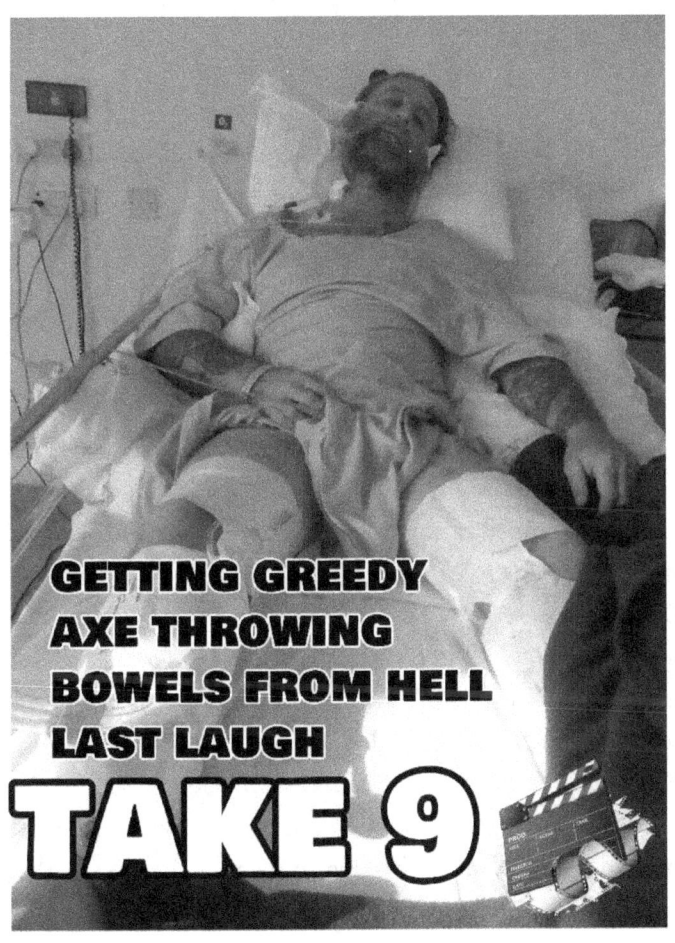

TAKE 9

The year 2015, proved to be a rather fruitful year for me, I had lots of film jobs. One afternoon, I received a call from Lady Marmalade. I wondered what she wanted and answered her call. She said, "Byron, I've got a job in India for you. Your profile has caught the director's attention, he wants you to play a Russian Mafia Don in his fantasy film." I replied abruptly, "Ok, if they want me to go there, I want five-star accommodation and full pay on my days off. I will need an assistant to prepare my meals every day. Please provide me with a written contract from both parties, otherwise I won't do it. I would like to fly directly to India, I don't want to fly on any of those crappy long-haul flights." I wanted to make it clear that I would not accept anything less than what I deserved. She answered, "OK, I'll get back to you tomorrow." I thought she wouldn't get back to me, since I was off with her and had been very blunt with my demands.

My phone rang the following day, while I was training. It was Lady Marmalade again. "Byron, I am pleased to say, that they have agreed to your terms. They want you at the Hyderabad film set, within the next six days. Send me your passport information and measurements." I replied, "OK, great. When I get back home, I will email you my details."

I was surprised that they accepted my conditions. It is common for Indian productions to ask for a discount and try to negotiate a deal, but they accepted the offer immediately. Preparations for my next adventure began. The details of the story were emailed to me shortly after. It read,

Several saints in India, predict the destruction of the Earth. They construct a sphere made from the strongest metals, which have the ability to absorb harmful UV rays, to protect the Earth. During a solar eclipse, the sphere must be kept at the Earth's equator. If one of the eclipses is missed, then the Earth will suffer major damage. The story moves to the present day, where a Russian don is plotting to capture the sphere so that he can hold the world to ransom and rule the world!

I thought this character, would be a fun part to play, especially in a fantasy film! After getting my gear ready for departure, I headed to the pharmacy for some Imodium, charcoal tablets, electrolytes and vitamins. I had been to India three times before and always had nasty stomach problems due to the food. This time though, I didn't want to make the same mistake of not having enough medication to control a volcanic diarrhea situation, so I went prepared.

A week later, I was on my way to the city of Hyderabad. The flight passed smoothly and I looked forward to my next excursion. The driver picked me up at the airport and drove me 45 minutes to Ramoji Film City. Spread over 1,666 acres of land. It is apparently the largest film studio in the world, according to the Guinness Book of Records. My hotel was situated within the studio grounds. I would be picked up at 8 a.m. the next day for my first day on set. I had an early night. The following morning, it took about 30 minutes to reach the filming location. When I arrived at the base camp, dozens of trucks, vans and trailers were shaded under trees. The site was approximately 20 acres of fields and jungle. I was surprised at how large the operation was. Production teams were scurrying around, carrying various materials to build the set. More than 200 people were working on it. An assistant who would work with me throughout the job greeted me. His name was Araav. My trailer was a converted truck trailer. It was pretty cool. It had a kitchen, dining area, showers and toilets. I chilled there while waiting for further instructions. After two hours, the assistant director called Araav to tell him to take me to the wardrobe to change. We proceeded to an old bus. This bus was a makeshift dressing room. The tents were to provide shade from the sun and protect us from the high humidity. The bus also provided a cooler area to change in, as the temperature outside was over 85°F.

I was passed a black suit by a tailor called Krishna. He was about three feet tall. I had never seen a tailor so small in my life. The suit was adorned with elaborate embroidery, giving it an expensive appearance. I was given a white shirt, Prada sunglasses, gold claw finger rings, a gold pocket watch, a hoop earring and a fake Rolex. "There is no doubt in my mind that you are a very wealthy man!" Krishna said. He was very proud of the wardrobe that he had sourced for me. The shoes were crazy, they were all gold and would have made Michael Jackson proud. After changing, Krishna proudly took a picture of me wearing my new outfit. He said, "The costume looks fantastic. The boss will be delighted." I was escorted to the set thirty minutes later. When I first saw the location, I was amazed. The attention to detail was remarkable. Every building, statue and hut was carefully crafted to look authentic and genuine. It was clear that a lot of thought had gone into making the city look and feel like a real African and Mayan village. It looked like something from *Fantasy Island*. I was impressed. The level of detail was astounding. Every detail, from the huts to the statues, was carefully constructed to be realistic. I was amazed that the crew had spent so much time and effort creating such a realistic set.

The director waved me over. Several of his assistants sat around him under a big umbrella. Fat, wearing a short-sleeved shirt, slacks and a Panama hat, the director looked like a mafia don. His microphone was in his hand. The crew waited for him to direct the next scene. Turning dramatically to me, he said, "You will play a wealthy, powerful man and you want to rule the world. To rule the world, you need the power that gives life to the world." He picked up a small brown, 4-inch-wide sphere with bizarre engravings on it. It looked like something from the *Lord of the Rings*. He went on to say, "If you have this, you are God. Remember that!" He was so convincing that I thought he should be there instead of me! Answering him, I said, "Wow that sounds amazing!" He replied proudly, "This is, without a doubt, the biggest film of the year in India." I answered back, "Is that true?" With a wink and a confident smile, he said, "Really!" It was the biggest film in India, but I had one major problem. I said, "Excuse me, sir, but I haven't got any lines!" The director replied, smiling,

"That's because we haven't written them yet!" I replied, "Oh," I nodded in agreement. My thoughts were, I am here now, earning a living and going on a business trip and in 3 weeks, I will be relaxing on a beach, soaking up the sun. So I'll do as I'm told. He's the boss. He knows what he's doing. That afternoon, I was called on set for a walking shot to introduce my character. I walked through the crowd of Ghanaians for my intro scene and that was that. Day one was over! I had dinner at the hotel restaurant, had a few beers and then retreated to bed early. So, I would have enough energy to play my ruthless character the next day! I was excited.

It was the big day. All eyes were on me as I returned to this amazing set. A plane had been constructed in the jungle, which was my private plane. As big as an Airbus, it had Russian insignia. In my first shot of the day, I had two of my henchmen standing near the plane. The name of one of them was Mambo! An imitation of *Rambo!* Originally from London, he wore paramilitary clothing. Since I had no lines given to me at that time, I reminded the assistant director. He said to me, "We will tell you about your lines over the microphone." There's a first time for everything when in India, do as the Indians do! So, I adapted to the situation. Different people have different ways of doing things. As a result, I just got on with it, I didn't have a choice!

I have worked on some Hollywood productions in the past and witnessed some actors forgetting their lines. So, the production wrote them on cardboard boards with an assistant holding them up! When we started filming my scene, they shouted me my lines over the microphone and I repeated what they said. All in all, I was amazed at how quickly and efficiently we were able to complete the scene. After another easy day, I was taken back to my hotel and celebrated with a beer and some tasty food, then straight to bed. I returned to the set, the next day to shoot some major fight scenes.

My previous encounter with the stunt coordinator on this film was in Bangkok, on another Indian production. I disliked him because he was rude and impatient. The production I worked on with him on before, was the Indian rip off version of *Taken*. The stunt coordinator and I glared at each other. I knew it would be fun! He would try to prove a point and put me through some hard-fight scenes.

He told me to go easy on the main Indian actor called, Khil. The next day, they needed to film Khil diving into a lake and jumping out with the sphere. It was an important plot point in the film. After putting on his stunt harness, he was connected to a stunt crane by a wire cable. Khil was hoisted into the air and submerged up to his neck. Action was called, the crane pulled him up in the air, making it appear as if he had jumped out of the water like *Spider-Man*. In a three-point stance, he landed safely. Therefore, making Khil look strong. In the shade of a tree, I sat with my assistant watching everything. It looked dramatic. It was time for some dialogue with him after he had completed his scenes. This involved a conversation, while I held him at gunpoint with a group of my henchmen beside me, including Mambo. I forced Khil to give me the sphere that he had just recovered from the bottom of the lake. We completed those scenes and then the start of my action sequences would be filmed after lunch.

It Ain't All Glitz & Glamour

We began filming the bulk of the action at, 2p.m. that afternoon. Meanwhile my right-hand man, Mambo and Khil engaged in a crazy gunfight. During this sequence, Khil, dodged Mambo's bullets with ease. Khil, then disarmed Mambo and smacked him in the head with a shovel. He then threw Mambo into a lake like a rag doll! To achieve this stunt, Mambo was attached to a stunt crane. It was funny to watch. He was dipped in and out of the water, like a fly fisherman casting his rod, into the stream for trout.

During the second sequence of this fight, I grabbed the sphere and began to take cover during the gunfight. I shot my pistol at Khil and hit him in the shoulder. In the background, a volcano erupted and I board my plane to escape. They cheated this shot by using a green screen behind my plane! During takeoff, Khil pulls himself together, despite being shot and like all heroes gets into a jeep and chases my plane down the runway. He then jumps on the wing of the plane. The stunt crane was used to accomplish this. This scene was copied by the stunt coordinator watching *Mission Impossible*! We filmed the last sequence aboard the aircraft. There was alot of choreography involved in the fight. A hydraulic platform supported the plane. The aircraft was surrounded by green screens. Outside, massive flood lights shone through the plane's windows. I shot at Khil with my pistol, he was hanging on the aircraft wing in the first part of the showdown attached to the stunt crane via a wire. My gun then ran out of bullets. As I tried to reload my gun, Khil then climbs onto the plane wing and enters the cockpit. After that, "Cut!" Was called.

We moved on to the final sequence of the airplane fight,

which was my death scene. Khil attacked me once inside the plane, pushing me back into the fuselage. The hydraulic platform then started to swing the plane from side to side. Khil then threw me onto a seat at the back of the plane. I front-kicked him off on the chest. He stumbled back. To spice up the fight, I conveniently found an axe near my seat. (*You only get this in the movies, trust me, as I have never seen an axe on a plane!*) I got up and threw the axe at Khil, nearly taking his head off, which he skillfully avoided. The axe flew towards the pilot's head and killed him, lodging itself in his forehead! The dead pilot slumped forward, then his limp arm pushed the control lever down and the plane nosedived. Then, "Cut!" Was called! Timing is everything when filming this type of sequence. My goal was to prove a point to the stunt coordinator. I got every shot in one take. With the pilot, they put in a separate take of him getting hit by the axe in the head by CGI. The axe I threw was a prop axe made from rubber.

That afternoon, I was hooked up to the stunt crane outside the plane. They hoisted me approximately 15 feet in the air and swung me around, so I was near the front door of the aircraft. Two cameras were set up. One was inside the plane and the other was outside, near the wings. This sequence began with Khil kicking me out of the door and I fell to Earth, dead and splattered. The coordinator was impressed and he shook my hand. My accomplishments made me proud, but I was completely drained by the time I got home that evening. After dinner, I went back to my room to settle in. After checking my emails, I set my alarm for the next morning. I eventually fell asleep. I was about to experience my worst nightmare! A couple of hours later, I woke up with the most horrific stomach pain, a high fever and I was shaking like a leaf. I suddenly felt like something was pushing its way out of my stomach. It was like the scene from Alien. The pain was unbearable. I screamed! I heard a bang on my wall. Next door, people shouted. "Be quiet!" I struggled to get up and went to the bathroom, where I collapsed on the floor. Then it began! World War III in the plumbing department.

It was the most violent projectile vomiting and shits I have ever experienced in my life! The chicken tandoori and rice I had been digesting that night went everywhere. It repeated itself every few minutes. It was terrifying for me. Laying there in agony, I felt nothing but pain. To wash the vomit and the red diarrhoea away, I turned on the shower. I heard the phone ringing. I knew it was a complaint from next door. Since I was too weak to get up, I didn't answer it. A knock came on the door five minutes later and someone shouted. "I would appreciate it if you kept your noise down, Mr. Gibson." I yelled back. "FUCK YOU!"

After that, I heard nothing more and slumped in the shower for two hours. I was exhausted. I cleaned myself up and lay on the bed, weeping like a wounded animal. To cork the blast from hell coming back, I took charcoal tablets, Imodium and paracetamol. After three hours, my alarm woke me at 7 a.m. After having a sore stomach and feeling completely shattered, I felt fragile. In the wake of vomiting, I developed a sore throat, but I overcame it and got ready to go to work. I thought it was just a one-time stomach issue. To get rid of the infection, I skipped breakfast that morning.

Within a few days, I thought I would be fine if I starved the virus. On arrival at the location, I felt lightheaded. I told the director and his assistants that I was feeling poorly. I stayed in my trailer most of the morning, waiting for them to call me.

After a while, there were some more movements in my stomach. The sensation was like a snake slowly moving around in a confined space, feeling its way around and looking for a way out. The situation deteriorated. The trailer door was then opened by my assistant. The timing was terrible. He said, "They need you on set in 10 minutes." I washed my face and put on my costume. I was trying to put a brave face on the situation. The sun was scorching outside. The midday sun only made matters worse, as I was already weak. On set, I strolled, trying to control the bells of hell in my stomach. Keeping my cool and remaining confident, I knew I could only hold off for a short period of time. There was a crowd of people waiting for me. In this scene, 300 extras from Ghana surrounded the main actor and me. Khil's entourage applauded, as he approached me. We faced each other, we exchanged glances. Trying to be professional, I smiled. He was waiting for me to begin the dialogue.

While I was trying to maintain a straight face, my stomach was imploding uncontrollably. I began sweating and huffing and puffing. For certain roles, actors perform animal exercises before their scenes. Khil probably thought it was my way of getting in the acting zone, so he let me get on with it. I saw a smile on his face. After taking a few deep breaths, I burped out loud. There was shock on Khil's face. The rolling of my stomach stopped. Standing straight, I regained my confidence.

The director and entourage were staring at me. As they waited for an Oscar-winning performance, I smiled and said, "OK, I'm ready."

I felt a hot flush come over me. Khil noticed something wasn't right and stepped back. I don't know what type of face I made, but he knew something bad was about to happen. It did! Whoosh! As I projectile vomited at him, just like a muck spreader spraying the fields. I fell to the ground, puking everywhere near his feet. It went on and on. Vomit rained down out of my mouth like a tsunami. As Khil walked back shaking his head, he couldn't believe what had just happened to him. This time, he did not receive a round of applause from his entourage. The Exorcist's director would have loved me! An eerie silence hung in the air. The crowd of Ghanaians started laughing. I was surrounded by evil eyes. The audience did not clap! The director came over to me and said with a pissed off tone, "You need to return back to your trailer."

I was picked up by two assistants and placed over their shoulders before being taken back to my trailer. The two of them tried to avoid my vomit on my clothes as we staggered back. I don't think they were happy fellows. Upon entering my trailer, I slumped on the toilet and it started again. It seemed to go on forever. It frightened me. This was the first time in my life that I had ever experienced something so severe. It felt like the room was spinning and I had the most intense headache. As soon as I got up from the toilet, I took two paracetamols. My body became weaker and weaker as I slumped on the bed and stared up at the ceiling. My condition began to deteriorate. I had a fever again and I was in the bathroom every 10 minutes. However, this time it was only liquid. After about an hour, I finally fell asleep.

I was woken by two clumsy fingers opening my eyelids. This guy looked down at me, flashing a torch into my eyes. The man resembled Groucho Marx. I asked him, "Who are you?" I glanced down at his case. It was filthy, like a mechanic's toolbox. He replied, "I am your doctor! I need to check your heartbeat." He reached for what appeared to be a Second World War stethoscope. I swear the plastic bits were baker-light! The stethoscope was placed on my chest and he tested my heart beat. He put the stethoscope away in the dirty black case, nodded to my assistant and then said, "We're taking you to the hospital, it's at least an hour away and you must go now. You are very ill." When I heard that, my heart sank. My mind was racing. Was I going to die on a movie set in India? I honestly wasn't sure if I was going to make it to the hospital on time.

As we were driving to the hospital, my driver weaved in and out of the traffic like a *Grand Theft Auto* player. I was barely holding up with my bowels. Every bump in the road affected my delicate stomach. Three or four times, I had to vomit out the window. I simply slid the side window open and let it go, there was no choice. I puked out the window, as we were being overtaken by a motorcyclist and it splattered him! It was all over his chest and helmet. He was so pissed off, shaking his fists at me. But what could I do? We arrived at the hospital after what seemed like an endless dodgem ride.

When the driver pulled up beside the Accident and Emergency Department, nurses ran to get me. After being placed in a wheelchair, I was rushed to a room with a female doctor. I had trouble understanding what she said. I had blurred vision and my head was spinning. Ten minutes later, I came around with two more doctors examining me. The doctor said, "We're moving you to another hospital, because we don't have the facilities to take care of you here, you could die." I then fainted. I woke up about 30 minutes later and was riding in a van through Hyderabad's congested streets. Then I passed out again.

In a new hospital, I came to on a stretcher, being pushed through many wards. My only memory is of a doctor, trying to wake me up. The feeling of weakness and disorientation was overwhelming. The doctor said, "Mr. Gibson, I'm taking you to the intensive care unit." He was holding some paperwork and pointing to the sheets of paper, with a pen in his hand. I asked, "What's that for?" He replied, "I need you to sign this Sir. Your life depends on it." I scribbled on the paperwork some kind of signature. That was all I could muster up, then again, I lost consciousness.

A beeping noise woke me up six hours later. I wore an oxygen mask and was attached to a life support machine. It was early in the morning. My attention was caught by a nurse who sat in a chair watching me. I asked her, "Where exactly am I? Are you able to speak English?" She smiled back at me! Unfortunately, she didn't speak any English. I was in an isolation room and my feet and legs were strapped with pipes. I was attached to a life support machine. I could barely move and could only stare back at her, feeling like I was in prison. My neck had a pipe inserted into it. I had an intravenous drip in my hand and arm. There was another tube inserted into my leg, just below my groin. When I tried to move, I had excruciating pain. I lifted the covers up and there was a pipe in my penis! It was a catheter! If you've ever had a catheter, you know it's not pleasant. The pain after it's been inserted hurts like hell. I was at such a low point that I had no idea where I was. No one spoke English, except the doctor I saw earlier. My mind was filled with terrible thoughts and I thought the end was near. Had I contracted a tropical disease? I had no control over my body. I was so weak; I could barely speak. My family had no idea where I was and I didn't know what was happening to me. My nurse came over with a towel to wipe my forehead. I then passed out again.

The next morning, I woke up with something prodding my right bottom cheek. Someone was digging their fingers into my backside. I was in a daze and thought, Jesus, I've been through all this shit and now Gary Glitter is here, trying to have is way with me! As I slumbered to my right, I noticed a young man who looked like Adrian Mole, wearing goggles, elbow-length black long heavy-duty industrial gloves and a boiler suit. He was opening my bottom cheeks and looking at my backside, as if he was looking for lost treasure! Obviously, I was enraged! I said to him, "What the fuck are you doing?" He jumped back and replied, "My job is to clean you sir." I was glad he could speak English. However, I was pretty upset about what he was doing. He went on to say, "I am sorry, Sir!" I replied, "You don't have to do that. I will let you know when I need to go to the bathroom. Now please put the bloody cover back down!" I then passed out again.

My nurse opened my curtains at 9 a.m. the next day. After that, she adjusted my bed so that I was sitting upright. She then gave me a cold glass of lemon juice. I gulped it down, like a man possessed, I was so thirsty. Soon after, a doctor approached my bed and stood over me. A smile spread across his face as he introduced himself. "I am pleased to meet you! Mr. Gibson, I am Dr. Anish Anand, head of internal medicine at Apollo Hospitals in Hyderabad. We met last night. I studied at an NHS hospital in Cardiff Wales and I speak English. I can assure you that you are in good hands." I replied, "I am pleased to meet you, Dr. Anish. Could you please tell me what is wrong with me?" He answered, "We do not know what is wrong with you right now and your case is extremely severe. We need to do some more tests for a diagnosis. For the time being, you need rest."

I was scared out of my wits when he told me that. The doctor held my hand. "Don't worry. My nurses are with you 24 hours a day. We have this under control. I'll be back this afternoon and my nurse, needs to take more blood, for the diagnosis test, if you don't mind." The doctor smiled and I replied, "OK." I look forward to seeing you this afternoon. The doctor waved to me and left my intensive care unit. Observing a park area from my room window, I slowly turned to my side. A nurse inserted a hypodermic needle attached to a syringe into my arm. A sample of blood was taken. I was given a lemon drink after she finished the procedure. My pillow was then buffed up and I was tucked in. With the blood sample in hand, she left the room. Despite my exhaustion, I somehow believed everything would be OK.

I was woken up by the nurse and the Dr. that afternoon. I was given another lemon drink by the nurse. As soon as I finished it, the doctor said, "I am glad you slept well. It is time for me to tell you what the problem is. Bacterial sepsis, hypotension, severe shock, acute renal failure, pulmonary odema and fever are the diagnoses." My first thought was blimey, what on earth have I contracted? Am I going to turn into a bloody zombie? I replied to the doctor. "Well, what does that mean?" The Dr. replied, "I will explain. Bacterial sepsis is the body's extreme response to an infection. Sepsis occurs when an infection triggers a reaction throughout your body. You have bacterial sepsis in your gastrointestinal tract, urinary tract and lungs. It's very extreme. This could be Escherichia coli, which you may know as Ecoli. You may get pneumonia. You may also have hypotension. Your body's vital organs are not getting enough oxygen and nutrients. They are shutting down; this is why you are in shock. Since you arrived in India, what have you eaten? Which kinds of restaurants have you visited?"

I replied, "I've only eaten food from the film set and the hotel restaurants. My assistant got my food from a nearby hotel." After that, the doctor said, "We think you have been infected by digesting human feces. It will take some time to improve, but you'll be fine in the end. More tests will be conducted. Oh, we need to know who will pay for your treatment while you stay with us." When I heard about human feces, I was angry and shocked. I was retching, I had literally eaten somebody's shit! I had to think quickly about who would pay the hospital bill. I didn't sign any insurance certificates for this job, only a film contract and I was uncertain if I was covered. I said, "The film producer will cover my hospital bills." The doctor answered, "Well, they have not contacted us. Don't worry. I will have my staff look into it. I will see you tomorrow." After the doctor left, I realised I had left my phone, money, passport, clothes and everything else at the hotel. I fell asleep at that point.

For days afterwards, I suffered from severe diarrhea, muscle cramps, dizziness and extreme fatigue. The noise from the life support machine, drove me up the wall with the constant beeping. I could only gaze out the hospital window and I still required assistance to go to the toilet. Whatever food they gave me, passed straight through me. The amount of lemon juice I drank, made me hate it in the end. I have never drank it again, despite its many benefits. After the fifth day, things began to change and I gradually became stronger. I was well taken care of by my medical team during my recovery. After the sixth day, the shits slowed down and eventually stopped. My bottom wiper was relieved! After the seventh day, I felt much stronger and was capable of walking without assistance.

I desperately wanted to contact Leigh in Thailand, but I had no phone, my passport, laptop, clothing and money was missing. My doctor came to see me for his regular checkup. During his visit, I told him about my missing items. The hotel I previously stayed in, then was notified by him. They told him, there was no sign of my belongings. Several days later, one of the film producers showed up with it out of the blue. Maybe they were playing games with me, so I couldn't leave. I felt so relieved. I told the producer I was going to leave India as soon as possible. I just wanted out of there. The producer said to me, "Your role in the movie is vital and you have to stay to finish it!" It's not possible to complete the film without you. You need to return to the set tomorrow to complete a sequence in the film." He was quite demanding. I didn't have the strength to do that. I shook my head and said, "No, way!" The doctor then jumped in and told the producer, "He cannot leave for another three days and you need to book him a flight back home immediately." After the doctor told him this, the producer left, pissed off.

Eventually, I got through to Leigh. As I hadn't contacted her, for all the time I was there, she was worried and wondered what was happening. She said she contacted Lady Marmalade, who said I was fine and still working on the movie and I just had a bad stomach. It didn't make any sense to me. There is no doubt that Miss Marmalade was aware of what was happening. In other words, she was bullshitting to keep Leigh happy. I told Leigh to expect me back within three to four days.

Two days later, the producer returned to the hospital, very concerned and eager to get me back on set. The other producers were putting pressure on him. He asked, "Would you like to spend another month in India?" I said, "No fucking way!" He pleaded with me. The poor me card, was being played by him. The doctor piped in and said, "He needs more time to regain his strength. It's impossible for him to work on a movie set, right now!" The producer was unhappy after hearing this. I thought, OK, I'd meet this guy halfway. I told him, "I will finish my dialogue scenes, but then I must return to Bangkok." He replied, "Why must you return home?" I replied, "It's obvious, you uncompassionate bastard. I nearly died!" He was being selfish and just cared about his stupid movie. He had completely disregarded my feelings and health and was just interested in getting what he wanted.

They needed me to complete my scenes at the beginning of the movie. So, I knew I had him by the balls. I said, "If you don't book a flight for me, I will do it myself." I was going to cut my losses and get the hell out of there. I said to him, "In four days, I will return to your film set to complete my filming, but only if you book me a flight home the same day. Pay me and sort the hospital bill out." He replied, "I agree." Four days after being released from the hospital, production picked me up and took me to the film set. Despite still not feeling well, I returned to work. I was exhausted.

My legs would get tired after a few minutes of walking. I had to be always assisted. I knew I only had one hour to film, then I would be on the way home. I struggled through the scenes. The atmosphere was unpleasant and all eyes were on me. I was the bad guy who was apparently fucking up on their film set. After doing my dialogue scene. I returned to my trailer and waited until my ride to the airport arrived. During this time, they brought me some food, I thought they were taking the piss, as I wasn't going to eat it! My lift took three hours to arrive. At this point, I did not have a flight ticket either, even though I knew I was supposed to fly at 7 p.m.

They were playing games with me and intended to keep me waiting, possibly even causing me to miss my flight. I got pissed off with one gormless twat, who was blanking me, when

I was asking where my lift was. I told him I would take a taxi to the airport and get my own flight, if he didn't book it. After that, he disappeared to inform his superior of the situation. A few minutes later, my lift arrived. The twat handed me my flight tickets, without saying a word. I said to him, "Where is my money?" He smiled at me and said, "No money." I left.

I arrived in Bangkok after three stopovers, I was exhausted. They had booked me on the longest flight back home, cheeky bastards. However, it was great to be back home again. Leigh was shocked at my appearance. My skin was greyish and I was so thin, she said, "You look like the walking dead!" My weight had dropped by five kilograms. The following days, I would usually be exhausted by 3 p.m. I would have to sleep until the next morning. My flight back to the UK was booked two weeks later. After undergoing a thorough medical examination and many tests in the UK. My doctor was amazed at what I had gone through. The diagnosis information I had received in India was given to him. I was told that my fitness had saved me and I was a fortunate man to have made it through. My doctor told me I shouldn't travel back to India for twelve months because if I got the infection again, I could die.

In reflection, I tried to identify the cause of my food poisoning. I used to get my food from the hotel's restaurant after filming, which was clean and upmarket. However, you never know what goes on behind closed doors. Perhaps the kitchen was filthy. There was a possibility that the chefs did not wash the vegetables or had dirty hands. I was told though my assistant got my food from a cheap street vendor and he pocketed the rest of the money. My lunch budget they gave my assistant was around 50 pounds a day. In India you can get a meal for a pound a day, so he probably did the dirty on me. By getting cheap food and pocketing the change. Several weeks passed. To my surprise, I received a bill from the hospital in India demanding that I pay for my hospital treatment. I couldn't believe it. The producers hadn't paid the bloody bill! I was treated so well at that hospital, so I was even more pissed off when I got the invoice. Up until that point, I hadn't been paid a penny for my work on the film. I believe they had no intention of paying me. I messaged the film producer, Vancat, who turned out to be a right slime ball. He said, "We are not paying you." I deliberately called him many times over many days, both early in the morning and late at night to bug him. However, he ignored my calls and never replied to my messages after that. I called him every morning between 2 and 3 a.m. Indian time for five days. I sent him around fifty voicemails. As a result, I put the film down as a bad experience and tried to move on.

Weeks later, things started to go my way. The universe works in mysterious ways. I was contacted again by Lady Marmalade. Her empathy was nonexistent. I received a message from her saying, "Byron, I know you are angry, but you shouldn't blame the Indian movie. Please let me know when you can come back to India for a one-day shoot. I will pay for your round-trip, by business-class airfare. The director and producer really need your help, to complete the project. There will be a half-day of shooting in a house. If you do not complete the film, I will lose face. They cannot finish the film without you. Help me, please. I am in a terrible situation!"

Karma is a bitch. I pulled out my Trump card. I responded, "I will complete the film for them. However, please settle the hospital bill first. Please send me the money they owe me for my work too. I need a screenshot of the payments, so when the payments are clear, we can negotiate." Then the cheeky bitch sent me this, "Make sure I receive my commission." What a greedy parasite, she was! I could have died over a stupid action movie and all she cared about was her money!

I waited patiently for the funds to reach my UK bank account. After five days, finally it arrived. The hospital bill was also paid. Then I got a call from Lady Marmalade. She said, "Byron, I am booking your flight as soon as possible. When will you be able to fly?" In response, I said, "Sorry. My doctor has told me, I cannot go back to India for at least 12 months and I am too weak to fly. Sadly, the film will have to be completed without me. Bye-bye!" I put the phone down. I smiled at myself. That was one of the most satisfying things I had done in a long time. Since the film was being written as it was being made, they could easily resolve the issue of me not being there. After the call, I received messages from Lady Marmalade and the producer, Vancat. As he did to me, I ignored his messages and blocked him. That was the end of the communication between us. I never had any business dealings with this greedy agent again. I knew I would be blacklisted.

I spoke to Equity, the Actors Union in the UK. They told me that if it had been a British or American production, I could have sued and claimed damages. They warned me never to work on a production like this again, because I was probably uninsured. They also told me that if I hadn't been paid, I could have stopped the film from being released in the UK by getting a judgement against them. I was pleasantly surprised when the film came out. The footage was cool, except for the first scene where I appeared in the movie. This was the scene, they needed me to complete. My face had been replicated by CGI and they put it on another guy's face with the same body size as me, so they could complete the film. I laughed at it. It was bizarre. The movie failed at the box office. With some of my payment from the film, I sent the nurses and the poor guy who wiped my bottom, some cash as a big thank you.

It Ain't All Glitz & Glamour

TAKE 10

It's strange in life how sometimes you can unexpectedly meet people who are famous out of the blue. So, when I strolled into an *Asahi TV* commercial casting, I figured it'd be another routine cattle call. Little did I know, I was about to walk into a scene straight from a John Woo film, the mastermind behind action classics like *Hard Target and Face/Off*. I didn't recognise him at first, but the man from Catalonia spotted him instantly. "That's John Woo!" he hissed; his eyes wide with excitement. He wasn't the imposing figure I'd imagined, but a small man with kind eyes and a mischievous glint. He moved with the quiet confidence of a seasoned warrior, his presence electrifying the room. The humdrum of the casting room suddenly seemed like a distant hum, replaced by a quiet buzz of excitement. John Woo, the legend himself, had seen our showreels. He saw something in us a spark of Western grit in me, a steely glint in the Catalan's eyes. He chose us. Two unlikely cowboys were handpicked to bring his *Asahi* commercial vision to life. It was an honour that resonated deep within, a feeling that transcended the usual casting call thrill. We weren't just actors anymore, in John Woo's eyes, we were his gunslingers, ready to step into the celluloid world he'd meticulously crafted. So, the next time you find yourself in a seemingly ordinary casting room, remember you never know who might be watching. You never know when your own John Woo moment, might be waiting just around the corner. My phone buzzed just as I was departing the *Asahi* casting room, a pleasant mix of post-audition adrenaline and anticipation for the shoot. But the call, from the producer of *Bareknuckle*, was a sobering reminder of the film industry's less glamorous side, where competition for resources can be fierce. The producer dropped some good and bad news.

The good news was the film was optioned by an American studio! So, things were shaping up, however, the bad news really pissed me off. The ghost writer who was working with us, wanted me out of the writing process and he wanted to take the credit for the story. He told the producer that I was not needed any more. Cheeky bastard. In the end, the producer dropped him and I wanted to drop him with my right hand. I couldn't comprehend that this muppet wanted to take all the credit for the creation when it was based on my true story. I was beginning to realise that the movie industry was a bright mirage, glittering with promise. However, peeling back the layers reveals a complex tapestry woven with ambition, desperation and yes, even loyalty. The film business, I was discovering, was a gilded cage where vultures always circled, ready to snatch a piece of the pie. Fame is a double-edged sword that is able to either illuminate or consume, depending on who wields it. It's a dance with the darkness, a high-stakes gamble where the price of success is often measured in betrayal. Despite this parasite upsetting the momentum, I cracked on with my mission and was back on track.

The time had arrived for myself and the Catalonian to begin our journey into the world of high-end TV commercials. What made this experience unique was the fact, that the filming was being approached as if it were a live movie set. I was chosen as the main outlaw, while we were tasked with causing chaos in a bustling marketplace, filled with countless extras and skilled stuntmen. The filming of the ad, spanned a full week, featuring drift cars speeding through a bustling market and careening madly through the stalls. Meanwhile, my partner, the Catalonian and I, would let off bullet rounds into the air, inciting utter chaos. The final scene resembled that of a Wild West showdown, reminiscent of *Blazing Saddles.* The ultimate confrontation would be between myself and the protagonist of the advertisement. He skillfully disarms me and delivers a fierce blow to my stomach, propelling me into the air.

Our initiation into training under the guidance of John Woo's esteemed stunt coordinators was a thrilling experience. The first scene we shot involved the cowboy's dramatic entrance into the bustling market with guns blazing into the sky. The coordination process was relatively straightforward, with the integration of stuntmen seamlessly among the extras in the crowded marketplace. As soon as we started firing, the panicked crowd scattered and the skilled stuntmen flawlessly executed their falls upon strategically placed boxes, tables and chairs. The rush of being a part of this exhilarating sequence was unmatched. In the afternoon, we moved on to the high-speed drift car scenes. The stunt coordinators had marked out designated safe zones for us, restricting our movement to avoid any accidents with the unpredictable cars. These drift cars would zoom into the lively market stalls, sending goods flying in all directions. With impressive precision, the cars would execute spins and donuts, adding to the chaotic yet captivating atmosphere. The sheer rush of adrenaline after just a minute of these intense stunts was electrifying. But with the help of the trained professionals, we braved through the choreography, emerging with a thrilling and dynamic sequence.

In the final showdown a few days later with the main protagonist. I draw my weapon and he expertly disarms me with a series of swift Kungfu moves. As if that's not enough, he proceeded to deliver a powerful kick to my stomach, causing me to be flung into the air and crash-land into a stack of boxes twenty metres away. As soon as the project was completed, we all gathered and raised our glasses of *Asahi* beer in celebration. Even John Woo, the renowned director, shook hands and praised our work, it would be the last time I would see him. Such is the nature of the movie industry, you spend countless hours working closely with your team and form bonds, only to be separated shortly after. The commercial was aired on Japanese TV and was a main feature in Empire magazine.

Following the advertisement directed by John Woo, I was presented with an array of exciting opportunities. One that caught my attention was called, *A Man Will Rise*. Featuring renowned Thai actor Tony Jaa and Hollywood action star

Dolph Lundgren. In this production, I played the deceitful accomplice Diego, to Lundgren's character. The setting, the Wild West. I devote an entire chapter in my second book to this film. Following the completion of my work on *A Man Will Rise*, I received offers for two other projects. However, as luck would have it, the shooting schedules for both projects coincided, leaving me with uncertainty about my availability. A conflict arose due to overlapping times and dates, creating a dilemma. *The Asian Connection*, starring martial arts icon Steven Seagal, was one of the films and I was to play one of the main antagonists. The other was a TV series called, *Brutal, A Taste of Violence*, starring Parkour founder David Belle. I thought sod it, I will try and do both. Some of the days overlapped. I worked on *The Asian Connection* during the day and *Brutal* at night.

Both projects were so important to me, because they had pages and pages of dialogue. Having to rehearse all the lines for two movies, was quite a challenge. My mind was all over the place at times and I was even dreaming of the characters. I had over 200 pages of script, which is a lot to master, with two completely different characters to contend with. I needed to give each project the attention it deserved, or else, I would be spreading myself too thin and would make myself look like an amateur. It was a juggling act, but I was determined to make it work. My involvement with the *Asian Connection* was a true delight, as the concept of robbing banks has certainly crossed all our minds at some point. In this production, I relished the adrenaline rush of riding a Yamaha 250cc trials bike through the urban streets, decked out in all black with a machine gun strapped to my back, reminiscent of a contemporary cowboy. As expected, we underwent rigorous firearms training and the skilled stunt coordinator, Keisha from Jaika Stunts, brought his expertise as an old-school stunt master to the project. His humility and exceptional talent make him stand out among other coordinators I have encountered.

In one scene of the film, I found myself behind the wheel of a Mercedes SL convertible, sipping on some whisky as I cruised down a four-lane motorway. The camera, positioned on the side of the road, captured my antics using a long lens. As soon as I hit the highway, I began performing my lines, accompanied by Jack the other actor and our second cameraman. As I glanced in my rear-view mirror, I noticed a police officer on a motorcycle, lights flashing, gesturing for us to pull over. I could tell the officer was ecstatic, probably thinking he had hit the jackpot. He was thinking who were these two foreigners driving down the highway, with a bottle of whisky in hand? The officer pulled up next to our car and motioned for us to stop. Shaking his head in disbelief, he spoke to me quickly, I couldn't make out what he said, but my first thought was, "Shit, I'm about to end up in the nick for drink driving." Little did he know, the whisky in my hand was tea!

To prove my innocence, I offered him a sip of my Whisky. He was taken aback, almost shocked, by my gesture. Dollar signs were lighting up in his eyes, he looked like he had won the lottery! I tried to pass the bottle to him again. My offer made him burst out laughing. But deep down, I feared, I had made a grave mistake. Was this going to land me in more trouble? The officer pulled out his pad, perhaps to write me a ticket or worse. He got on his radio and was requesting some backup. He spoke to one of his colleagues, saying that he had just stopped two stupid guys in a Mercedes convertible, driving down the highway and drinking a bottle of whiskey. His partner laughed on the radio.

Our walkie-talkie came alive and saved the day. The director's assistant on the other end of the radio, asked me what the copper was doing. I said to them, I think he's going to arrest us. The assistant told me to pass the radio to him. I told the policemen to speak with the production I was working on. He looked confused. The road wasn't blocked off and I'm not sure if the production had alerted the authorities that we were filming in the area. In seconds, everything was transformed. The officer relaxed, as he scanned our surroundings, taking note of the cameras cleverly positioned along the thoroughfare, meticulously capturing our every action. With a swift motion, he stowed away his notepad and registered that the man in the rear seat wielded a Steadicam. A look of disbelief crossed the officer's face and I suspect he believed himself to be a participant in some sort of *Candid Camera* prank. I cannot say with certainty, whether he comprehended that we were in the midst of filming a motion picture. With an apologetic bow, he acknowledged our presence, glanced around one last time and then resumed his journey. I put my foot down and drove off like the *Dukes of Hazzard.*

At this point in my career, I had achieved my desired status, by playing the bad guy doing both action and acting. I was a paid actor and enjoying the ride. Honestly speaking, I have never aspired to be the lead in a production. I have always relished portraying the antagonist and in this movie, I was robbing banks on dirt bikes, recklessly navigating through markets on motorcycles and engaging in shootouts with the police. Something we guys dream of. In another life, I think I would be a bank robber, if I could get away with it. The role posed a challenge for me, as I had to learn how to perform new stunts and learn a lot more dialogue in a matter of weeks. It made me emerge even stronger. I felt like I could accomplish anything. Now you're probably wondering how I got along with Steven Seagal. The icon is apparently known for his bad boy antics on the movie sets, but unfortunately, I didn't meet him on this film due to my schedule. As soon as I wrapped on *The Asian Connection*, I was on *Brutal*. I had no time to hang around, but I would meet Steven a couple of years later, where I would play his right-hand man in an action film in Manilla called *General Commander*.

Brutal, a 12-part television series produced by Studio Plus, a sister company of Canal Plus, was a challenging project for me. The early mornings and late nights pushed me to my limits. However, I was honoured to be part of the cast, as the producers and director had noticed my performance in *Only God Forgives* and believed I could bring the same level of brutality to my character, Marcus Knox. Playing a corrupt fight promoter, Marcus Knox was a complex character that I was able to bring to life with my understanding of the fight industry and its motivations. Having had personal experiences with deceitful promoters back in the day, I was able to portray Knox with authenticity and depth. It was one of those moments where I could draw on my life experience from all the arseholes I've met and put them into my character.

I believed I was this motherfucker, Marcus. Every moment spent in his skin was a thrill, a testament to the trust the producers had placed in me. But it was not just personal gain that drove me, I was determined to ensure success for myself and the production team.

We filmed all around Bangkok at some great locations. One night we were filming on a massive ship docked along the Chao Phraya River. It was a thrilling experience. The three hundred extras and skilled fighters provided the perfect backdrop for the story and my character. Utilising a skull with a GoPro attached as a microphone, I was able to immerse myself in the production and create an exciting atmosphere. My voice and announcing style were inspired by the legendary Michael Buffer, adding to the intensity of the show. As we filmed from 8 p.m. to 2 a.m. tour boats passed by, mistaking the fight scenes for an illegal match. It was a surreal experience, almost like a scene from a Charles Bronson movie. My role as a showman in *Brutal* was a dream. The thrill of performing on a ship, with tourists taking photos and watching the fights, added to the exhilaration of the show. As Marcus Knox, I was a son of a bitch and I loved every moment of it.

During the filming, we had the opportunity to shoot at Penang 96, a Muay Thai gym situated in the heart of a slum area called Klongtoey. This gym is located under an unyielding underpass, next to a set of railway tracks. The neighbourhood

It Ain't All Glitz & Glamour

is known for its rawness and the gym boasts some of the toughest fighters I've ever seen. To my surprise, the head trainer at the gym was none other than Master Peng, whom I recognised from Sor Thanikul, where he also held the position of head trainer. It was a serendipitous moment to see him again after all these years. Interestingly, Master Peng had a role in the film *Kickboxer*, portraying the head trainer whom Jean-Claude confronts when asking to fight Tong Po.

The leading actors of Brutal was David Belle and my old foe from *Only God Forgives*, Vithaya Pansringarm. Belle was a captivating individual and the genius behind the creation of Parkour. Belle's tenure in both the armed forces and the fire department contributed to his development into a multifaceted individual. While serving in the Marines, he achieved the esteemed feat of setting the record for rope climbing within the Forces and was duly recognised for his exceptional gymnastic talents. As I reminisce on a particular scene shared with him, my character is met with a forceful grasp around the neck, leaving me in awe of his immense strength and determination. The moment his hands grasped me, reality hit like a truck, bringing to life the authenticity of our connection. The camera captured it all, showcasing the beauty of our genuine interaction.

In the span of a mere two months, I had successfully worked on a 12-part television series and a feature film. Such a feat seemed incomprehensible from the outset, but I persevered. The arduous task of memorising all those lines of dialogue appeared to be an insurmountable mountain, yet I conquered it. This serves as a testament to the notion that, with determination, anything is possible. Unfortunately, I received a call from the producer of *Bareknuckle*, informing me that the American studio that had acquired the rights to the film would no longer be able to produce it and thus, the project was returned to our hands. It was a disappointment after all the anticipation, but such is life. I decided to put *Bareknuckle* on hold and divert my focus to other endeavours.

I carried on working and then out of the blue, I received a call from the production of *Brutal* a few months later. They asked me if I could play a free diving coach, as they had a job in Monaco. The role all depended on whether I could free dive. When I heard Monaco, I said yes! Even though I had never free-dived in my life! I thought I could train in the weeks before. Always remember, never say no to anything the universe brings! Rod, my mate from the markets, always said to me, never say no. After years of portraying villainous characters in films, I landed an exciting opportunity to play a new role in my filmmaking career. In my school years, my portly, pie eating careers teacher who donned frumpy corduroy attire said to me once, "Byron, you will never amount to anything." Despite his pessimistic words, I have triumphed and proven that fat arsed sugar blob wrong!

Angelo's was a free-diving coach in the series and his job was a big one. I needed to become proficient at free diving, but I also needed to be able to mentor and lead by example! I would be working as a coach with Caterina Murino, a gifted actress and former Bond girl from *Casino Royale*. I knew it was going to be a big task, but I was determined to succeed. So you're probably wondering how, on earth, I started training

It Ain't All Glitz & Glamour

for free diving. Well, it was quite simple. I read how to do it. First, I learned how to hold my breath through dry training. Which is quite a simple method by just laying on your back and holding your breath in a relaxed state. I learned about carbon dioxide and oxygen. Every day, I would spend a few hours in our pool and hold my breath. Over the weeks, I managed to hold my breath for up to two minutes. I read about the mentality of free divers and why they wanted to do it. It opened a whole new world to me, which I found fascinating. The production told me, I needed to be able to swim 20 metres down with no problem and there would be a lot of underwater shots. I had lots of dialogue and it was an amazing experience. One night we went out and the bill came to over 1,000 Euros, I can see why they call it the millionaire's playground.

After my month-long stay in Monaco, I embarked on a new project in China that proved to be a complete contrast. My accommodation was limited to a shabby and smoke-filled hotel and the food left much to be desired. However, the movie set was a stunning sight to behold. A sprawling industrial complex had been intricately transformed into a filming location, with each street representing a different city. Paris, New York and a war zone and more. Upon completing that project, I flew to Melbourne, Australia, to finish filming the period drama gangster film. After this, I returned to the United Kingdom, where I was cast in a 12-episode television series by Studio Plus, filming in South Korea and Belgium, portraying Marcus Knox again in *Dragon Race*. Thanks to the success of *Brutal*, I was chosen to play Marcus Knox once again, in a fantastic opportunity to showcase my skills on two separate TV productions, as the same notorious character. I was truly in my element, embodying the villain. Unhesitatingly accepting every booking that came my way, I was immersed in a sea of projects. An invitation from an action movie unexpectedly presented itself.

They were searching for an actor to play Steven Seagal's dependable ally in the film. This time, in contrast to my earlier experiences, I would be booked to play Tom Benton, an anti-hero. This movie, *General Commander*, was a good part with lots of dialogue, action-packed fight scenes, RPG battles against helicopters and much more. As I worked on the project more, I had the privilege of collaborating directly with Steven. When I first met him, it was clear that he had a thorough understanding of weapons. His proficiency with handling a gun was impressive and he demonstrated precise body movements while doing so. He treated them with the respect they deserved. Reports of Steven's rebellious actions on set had circulated, but with me, he was nothing but respectful. In fact, we formed an unexpected bond. We were booked to do a professional job and that is what we did. The cast and crew went out one night and we got to know each other a lot better. It was a group bonding session. Steven talked about the days when he started out in Hollywood. I didn't know it at the time, but he can speak a multitude of languages. He's fascinated by martial arts. Back in the day, his films made millions. Now you are probably wondering if he can still do his Aikido and based on what I have experienced with him, I would say 100 percent yes. The guy has hands like a vice and he would easily break your wrists. He still trains and teaches and he was training while we were in Manila.

David Gray, a former Marine Commando for *General Commander*, provided me with professional firearms training. He taught me numerous tricks of the trade and demonstrated how to properly use firearms and invade a building. We were filming one night on the Jones Bridge, which connects to Manila's Chinatown. In this sequence, Steven and I would ride in a black sedan to track down one of the crooks we were hunting. We're held up by a chopper that flies overhead and fires at us. We jump out of the car to fire back at the helicopter, but instead of using a rifle, I use an RPG, which knocks the helicopter out of the sky. This scenario was filmed in a unique way. The rocket I was shooting in the RPG had a wire attached to it so that it could safely launch into the river below, after rising into the air. It functioned essentially like a trace wire. As my finger pulled the trigger on the RPG, the first shot was unleashed, unleashing a burst of flames from the rear of the rocket. Instantly, my beard caught fire from the rocket emitting sparks and leaving behind a dark spiral of smoke. The burning and steaming sensation in my facial hair was a shocking experience. Quickly, I set the RPG down and checked my beard, which thankfully remained unharmed but carried a dreadful scent and showed signs of light burns. To say it was unexpected would be an understatement. My mouth was filled with the residue of gun powder, leaving my teeth coated in black. The make-up department soon arrived to clean me up and I couldn't help but chuckle at the absurdity of the situation. We went back for a reshoot once we had cleaned up. This time, however, a perspex guard was attached to the RPG to protect my mouth, eyes and beard. I shot the rocket and then exclaimed, "Merry Christmas, mother fucker." This was the best line in the entire film.

The coordinator stopped me during the last few takes of shooting the RPG. At the end of the bridge, a motorbike came along with a pillion passenger. They had passed through the barricades and appeared to have done a robbery in the city. They halted and stared intently at us at the other side of the bridge. In the background, an overturned automobile blazed fiercely. I don't think they understood we were shooting a movie. Their interpretation of this chaotic scene must have been bewildering, especially with me holding an RPG and my co-stars wielding submachine guns. But as they advanced towards us, I aimed the RPG in their direction. Startled, they abruptly did a u-turn and attempted to flee, only to be swiftly seized by the authorities. I worked on that film for one month, it was a great experience. After that film, yet again, it was the last time I saw much of the cast and crew, including Steven Seagal. I eagerly awaited the arrival of new projects. However, as time progressed, the flow of projects began to dwindle. Unfortunately, some of the promised projects never materialized. The thought of experiencing a lull in my busy schedule, something every actor dreads, crossed my mind. It was the start of a bad patch for me.

It Ain't All Glitz & Glamour

TAKE 11

Not everything in the acting game smells of roses. You need to be a tough cookie to survive the ups and downs of the film business. She will build you up and quickly knock you down. The problem with being an actor, is that you do not know when your next gig is coming. The business is completely unforgiving, which can sometimes be amazing and yet utterly demoralising. You need to possess a solid amount of savings to fall back on, unless you were born with a silver spoon in your mouth. A survey by the Queen Mary University of London, showed that only two percent of actors make a living from the profession. Eight percent are part-time and ninety percent are out of work. So, the odds of making it in the acting business are poor. There's no business-like show business! It's like a game of Russian roulette. The odds are against you, but if you're lucky, you'll be one of the winners.

My bank balance needed to be higher. I hoped another big gig was coming up soon. I was suffering from a histamine intolerance problem. Headaches, nasal congestion and sinus issues plagued me. I was frustrated, because no film bookings were coming in. I would usually find out about gigs, two to three months in advance. There was nothing in sight, not even a whisper. It was the most frustrating time I had ever had in the film world. After years of travel and good times, I was experiencing a quiet period. This was particularly challenging for me because I had become accustomed to a certain level of success. I felt lost and uncertain about the future. I turned on my computer that evening, hoping for an email from an agent, to tell me I would get some work. I anxiously sifted through my emails. I was about to close my Gmail account when an email popped up. It read, "Hello, Byron, I'm David Ready. I am Ready Entertainment's Executive Vice President of Film and Entertainment. A Chinese producer and many others in the industry have recommended you to me. Do you think you would be interested in casting for a film that I have in Indonesia? Best Regards, David Ready."

My wishes had come true! I jumped on it straight away. I checked out his email address and his company links. I received a link to his bio and the films IMDB listing. David was a producer from the USA, who had produced dozens of best-selling films. I had been contacted by numerous producers and directors via email throughout my career in the past. You can't rely solely on your agent, to get you work in the film industry. You must put yourself out there, chase after opportunities and hustle. Networking and self-promotion are paramount, for anyone looking to break into the film industry. It's essential to create a personal portfolio and brand. Then you have to reach out to potential employers with well-crafted emails. This is like looking for a job, you can't simply sit back and wait for someone to come to the door. You must put effort into marketing yourself to potential employers, sending well-crafted resumes and cover letters and networking with the right people. I would send out emails, every three months, offering my services to different productions and I thought this was a reply from one of them. Immediately, I typed, "Hello, David. That sounds very interesting. It would be helpful if you could tell me more about the film, the budget, the actors and the role you would like me to play. Thank you for your time. Yours sincerely, Byron Gibson."

David was in Los Angeles and there was an eleven-hour time difference between Thailand and the USA. I received a reply several hours later. "Hi, Byron. Thank you for your prompt reply. Find attached the film's synopsis below. Can we arrange a Skype call to talk things through further? Regards, David." He sent me a full breakdown of the movie, including the characters involved and shooting locations. I wrote back, "Hi David, No problem, 5 p.m. Thai time today. Best Regards, Byron." That afternoon, I eagerly awaited the call. After sitting at our dining room table, I turned on Skype and saw a friends request from David. Within seconds, I accepted and the call came through.

David answered, "Hello, Byron, I'm David Ready. I am pleased to meet you." He had an American accent. He sounded like he came from Queens, New York. I replied, "Pleased to meet you too, David." I couldn't see him. There was only a blank screen on my laptop. I could hear him sighing and tapping his keyboard in the background. I wondered what was going on. He sounded confused. "I'm here now, Byron. Can you see me?" I said, "No, not yet. What's wrong?" I could hear he was pissed off. He replied, "And now?" I could see nothing just the blank screen again. I replied, "Still nothing, David." I didn't want to be rude and ask him if the camera was on! David said to me, "This is so embarrassing. I have a bloody camera problem! I'm not sure what's wrong with it and I do apologise. I don't mind if you want to reschedule the call for another time. I don't like to do business like this. I can call you via WhatsApp, or we can do this on Skype, without the camera. Are you OK with that?" I replied, "Not a problem. Let's do it on Skype now." David replied, "Thank you, Byron." I turned off my laptop's camera and our conversation began. David said, "Please forgive me again for my camera not working. I told my staff to fix it last week. It seems temperamental. You would think an Apple laptop would be faultless, but no! I have had so much trouble with this one!" I replied, "It's not a problem."

I wanted to close the deal as soon as possible and get on with it. David spoke in a happy tone, "OK, great. Several sources have highly recommended you. In fact, six people have recommended you to me. Let's get down to business, as I am sure you want to know why I am contacting you. The film is based on an ex-mercenary named Gary Goldman. He served in the SAS and has turned rogue, forming his own group of mercenaries based in Indonesia. He kidnaps a rich businessman's wife and holds her for ransom. I want you to audition for Gary. Alicia and one of your co-stars from General Commander told me, you fit the role perfectly. As you are in Thailand and Jakarta is just a few hours away, you are the ideal guy for the role. I replied, "Thank you, David. Yes, I live between London and Bangkok." David replied, "That's great! The movie will be shot in Indonesia in the next twelve months. I have seen your showreels and I love them. The role fits your profile perfectly. I have been told you can arrange for a stunt team and get military advisors. Is that correct?" I was excited to hear this. I replied, "I would love to audition and if you require stunt people and military personnel, I can arrange this. Please tell me more."

I was confident, I could pull off a double whammy. I devised a quick plan. I could easily assemble a team of stunt performers for the movie, utilising my professional network. Also, I could get my friend Frank in Marbella, to be a military consultant. I needed to act fast. David responded, "When can you come to Jakarta to audition?" I replied, "Well, I'm free to audition anytime. I can fly to Jakarta whenever you want." David replied, "That sounds awesome. I'll have some of my team send you the script so you can self-tape it. Can you please send me your CV? I will forward it to my casting director, Sarah Finn. This is a highly confidential film, so please do not share it with anyone. The budget is substantial and the actor list is impressive. You will need to sign an NDA for us to proceed. You will receive an email with the complete contract details and script. As there is only a limited amount of time remaining, I need to speak to another actor who's auditioning. I will let you know about the stunts we require, on the next call. Please email me back as soon as possible and I will be in touch shortly." I replied, "Thank you, David. Have a great day and thanks for considering me."

I remember at the time, that there was a lot of activity going on in Indonesia in the film world. *The Raid* had put those guys on the map down there and I knew that quite a few guys had taken trips down to Jakarta, even though they kept tight-

It Ain't All Glitz & Glamour

lipped about it and their cards close to their chests. One thing I always remember is that they never talked about filming there, or how the projects turned out. This is likely due to the fact that Indonesia is still a relatively untapped market in terms of film production and they didn't want to give away any contacts or lose their competitive edge. However, it would be my first time working in Indonesia and I was looking forward to travelling there. I emailed my resume and sent a video of some of my work. I wanted to make sure that I was able to stand out from other applicants and that I had the best chance at getting the job. I also wanted to ensure that I was familiar with the company and the person I would be working with, so I did more research on David's company and Sarah Finn.

David sent me an email 48 hours later. He wrote, "Hello, Byron, The resume, photos and show reel were well received by Sarah and thanks for signing the NDA. I am pleased to inform you that you are now in the final stages of the casting process. If you send me your cell number, I will call you later today." So I sent David my cell phone number and asked him to call me eight hours later. That afternoon, I had just gotten home from shopping when my phone rang. It was a call from Los Angeles. It was David. "Hi, Byron, how are you doing today?" I replied. "Yes, I am doing well, thank you, David." David answered, "I have some good news to share with you. Congratulations! You have now made it to the final ten actors to audition for the role. Sarah liked what she saw! Could you fly to Indonesia to cast in a week? Your flight will be covered and you will stay in a luxurious hotel in the centre of Jakarta. We will give you 2,000 dollars for the week's compensation, for your professional services. Our requirement is for you to stay for 4-5 days to quote the action scenes. In addition, we want you to do your casting with Sarah." I replied, "Yes, David, that's not a problem."

David replied, "Ok, fantastic. Please bring a small camera and tripod, so you can audition and make previs videos, so you can send them to Sarah. Because bringing large film equipment into Indonesia at this point may attract import taxes. I will send you a breakdown of some of the scenes involving the stunts after this conversation. Embarking on a film project in Indonesia, requires careful preparation and an understanding of local regulations and cultural nuances. You understand that, Byron?" I answered, "Yes, David.

David replied, "You'll be escorted to the locations with a local fixer, to price the job and every location requires a permit, all of which my fixer has taken care of on the ground. You'll need permits for filming, especially in public and culturally sensitive areas. Even though some English is spoken in the cities, local fixers are invaluable for communicating in more remote and rural areas. Upon arrival, you will need to get to work as soon as possible. Time is of the essence. To begin preproduction on this film, we need to book all the locations within two weeks. I will be in Jakarta with my team in a few days."

I answered. "Thank you, that sounds great." David replied, "You will be competing against some of the best, for the role of Gary. I guarantee we will use the stunt team you recommend, if you give us a competitive quote. There will also be other actors, action advisors and clients there at the same time. Please don't speak with any of the other coordinators while you are there. They are your competition."

I replied, "Thanks, David. I'm looking forward to meeting you and auditioning. Pricing the stunts isn't a problem." David sounded happy and replied, "Byron, our research has found you to be highly recommended. Several producers have recommended you, as well as many actors and an American Asian stunt coordinator. Honesty and value are invaluable to me. Once again, thank you very much. I look forward to seeing you in Jakarta soon. In the next few minutes, my receptionist will send you an email that you should reply to ASAP." I replied to David, "Thank you. It will be a pleasure to work with you." I knew as soon as I put the phone down that I had a good chance of landing the role and the stunt job as well. I have gotten most of my work through recommendations. Therefore, whoever recommended me did me a great favor. I was already halfway there. Jakarta, here I come!

A few days later, I flew to Jakarta. From Bangkok, the flight took only three and a half hours. David's receptionist emailed me a few days before and told me that my pick-up would take place just outside the airport, near the parking lot, to avoid the crowds. Upon exiting the main entrance of the airport, I was met with a barrage of freelance taxi drivers, all vying for my attention and asking where I needed to go. It was overwhelming, to say the least. Then my eyes fell on the coffee shop and I saw the fixers waiting for me. They were quite an odd pair, to say the least. But I must admit that the film industry is full of strange people! It was like fatty and skinny! There was one who was overweight, with a mouth that stretched from ear to ear, like Zippy from Rainbow. In contrast, the other was skinny, with sagging grey jeans that revealed his cheap-market GT underpants. They certainly stood out from the crowd. The skinny fixer was trying to grow a beard, but it looked like he couldn't manage it. He had weird patches of hair on his face that looked like small tornadoes had been swirling around in them. Both held up a sign that said, Byron Gibson Ready Entertainment.

I walked over, introduced myself and shook their hands. The skinny fixer with the cowlick beard spoke English. He said to me, "It is a pleasure to meet you, Mr. Gibson. My name is Banyu and I'm your local fixer. I hope your flight went well. You have a very tight schedule. You will be taken to your hotel for freshening up before we head to our first location outside the city." I replied, "Pleased to meet you, Banyu." He replied, "This is your film permit. Keep a copy for yourself and send a copy to Mr. Ready." I thought it was strange as he didn't introduce the driver. While our conversation was in progress, the driver coughed a lot. Sadly, it sounded like he had bronchitis. Because Banyu didn't tell me his name, I will call him Kepala Kotoran. I said to Banyu, "Ok, let's get going." Knowing I would only be in town for a few days, I had to get down to business as soon as possible. I was going to be super busy doing the casting and pricing up the stunt job.

I have seen bad traffic in Thailand and India, but traffic in Indonesia tops them both. Jakarta is ranked seventh among the world's most congested cities and let me tell you, you have to see it to believe it. The traffic was so bad that it took us two hours to get to the hotel. Banyu checked me in. I settled into my room on the 12th floor and was immediately struck by the pollution over the Bay of Jakarta. I was told it was one of the smoggiest cities on the planet and they were right. After unpacking my gear, I decided to grab a quick snack and a coffee before heading out to meet Banyu. Unfortunately, Banyu had to report back to the office, but he assured me we would meet up later at the location. I followed Kepala to the car and we began our journey towards the first shoot location. It was around 2 p.m. so it was already late and I knew we were pushing it, but we needed to get down to business.

After three and a half hours in the car, I felt like I was suffocating. The car was an old banger and had no air conditioning. The sweltering heat and exhaust fumes affected my histamine problem. I was agitated after being stuck in terrible traffic. The combination of this journey and my flight from Bangkok took its toll on me. I had been travelling for quite a few hours until then. The traffic was at a snail's pace and I didn't think we would get to the location before dark. Outside, the traffic seemed never-ending, with motorcycles weaving through narrow gaps, street vendors manoeuvring their carts and the constant blaring of horns filling the air. It was as if honking was a common language among the drivers. Everyone vented frustration about the slow-moving traffic. Kepala didn't speak much English. He coughed constantly without putting his hand over his mouth. To find some relief, Kepala decided to spit out the window. He had no shame. I asked him, "How far is the location?" Kepala replied, "Thirty minutes." All I wanted was to get out of the sardine can and stretch my legs. I was losing my patience and was about to tell

Kepala, to go back to the hotel. However, David called me, it was such a relief. "Byron, its good you arrived safely. Banyu, told me you were on your way to the location. Please scout the area and see what you think. I need a breakdown of the stunts ASAP. An intro scene needs to be filmed in the jungle area for your character and a previs video shot. Take some photos, make an introduction tape for Sarah and report back." I replied. "Yes, David, the bloody traffic is terrible right now. We haven't reached the location yet. I hope we make it before dark." David replied. "I am aware that traffic is a mess down there, because I was there with the team two months ago, but please bear with me. However, Indonesia's locations are amazing. I'll fly there personally with my entire production team in five days. Work with my team on the ground in Jakarta. Please report back to me tonight, when you have completed what needs to be done. There are ten thousand Hindu temples in and around Jakarta and we have chosen the finest to film at. It took a lot of negotiation. The Hindu shrine you are about to visit is so visually impressive that you will be awestruck. Despite its World Heritage status, we're allowed to film there. Let me know what you think of the location." I replied, "OK, David, no problem. It sounds exciting. I look forward to speaking with you soon."

The call lifted me. Tired but excited, I eagerly awaited filming at these new locations and getting my hands dirty with a new project. Especially at a World Heritage site. I was confident I could land this gig easily. I told myself I needed to be more patient. Rome wasn't built in a day. Eventually, the driver took a slip road off the congested motorway and we left the traffic behind. We arrived at the first location. The Hindu temple was impressive, carved from stone and the surrounding area was dense jungle. We parked up and I followed Kepala to the temple. A caretaker greeted us, as I was guided through some stone-carved arches. The caretaker was an old, frail man with a warm smile. Despite his frail appearance, he walked with a sprightly step and seemed to know every nook and cranny of the temple, like the back of his hand. Kepala and the temple caretaker conversed in Indonesian. They seemed to agree as they continued their conversation. I couldn't understand what they were saying, but I noticed Kepala handing the caretaker some money, before they parted ways. Perhaps it was a token of appreciation for the caretaker's assistance, or maybe it was payment for something entirely different.

The caretaker must have been excited that a film was shooting there. The location was great, a cameraman's dream and they made an excellent choice. It was a masterpiece of architecture. With its intricate carvings and designs adorning its walls and pillars, it was awe-inspiring to witness such a grand structure, amidst the lush greenery of the jungle. It was a spiritual and peaceful experience and it was worth the long journey to get there in the end. I decided to film an introduction video outside the temple. I had some notes from David. They said, "Gary would be held up in the temple with his team of mercenaries. They are hiding from a military parole searching for the kidnapping victim." I scouted the locations for possible scenarios, looked at ways to shoot it and how many people we would need to form the mercenary team.

It took about two hours, but I finally had a solid plan in place. Kepala suggested we head back to the hotel since it was late. Banyu didn't show up and didn't even call to tell us why. We returned to the hotel just before 9 p.m. after a long and exhausting journey.

Kepala, pulled up near the hotel entrance. We were greeted by two greasy motorcycle guys, who looked like wannabe gangsters. It looked like they were trying to impersonate the Mexican MS-13 gang, but they didn't realise they were 10,000 miles away in South America. Both were smoking a cigarette each. Their leather jackets were adorned with various biker's patches that didn't make any sense. I think they bought whatever looked cool at the local market and sewed it to their jackets to appear more menacing. Their hair was messy and unkempt. The first guy had a greasy beard, he revved up his engine on his disappointing 125cc Honda Varo, causing smoke and noise to fill the air. He seemed proud of that hair dryer! The second guy, sporting a greasy pompadour hairstyle and a bandanna wrapped around his head, smiled as he approached us. He walked like Fonz, from Happy Days. He strutted with an exaggerated toughness and a fag in his mouth. He looked at me up and down and smiled, then shook hands with Kepala. Their poser attitudes were evident. They tried to have a tough guy persona but lacked the true grit and authenticity of real outlaw bikers. I kept walking and had no time to make new friends with these twats. As I entered the hotel, I looked back. The wannabe bikers smiled at me and I waved back to be polite. I just wanted to crash. It had been a long day stuck in traffic and I was drained. The constant stop and start of traffic took its toll. I was looking forward to decompressing with some rest and relaxation. Despite the long day, I knew it was worth it in the end. After a day of adventures, flying thousands of miles around Southeast Asia, being stuck in traffic in one of the most polluted cities on earth and ending up at a World Heritage Site. I was shattered. After ordering food, I ate my fried rice, sent the videos off and my reports to David and was out like a light.

The day came to travel to my second location. I headed down to breakfast and grabbed a coffee. Two other Westerners, around my age, also had breakfast. We exchanged smiles and nods before they sat down nearby, discussing a movie. It was clear from their conversation that they were part of the production crew. I assumed that they were also there for the same film as me, which meant that they were my competition for pricing up the stunts. I said, "Are you guys here for the movie?" One of them replied to me and said, "Yes." As I passed by them, they seemed to be aware of the non-disclosure agreement. They didn't want to speak much.

As I walked to the hotel check-in desk, I noticed Kepala waiting for me. Standing beside him was a French photographer with bags filled with camera equipment and a tripod. I assumed he was there for auditions and stills for the film. I approached Kepala and let him know I needed to grab my backpack before we could leave. The French photographer greeted me with a smile and we exchanged pleasantries. After a few moments, Kepala explained in broken English that the French photographer was a crew member. When I returned from my room, the photographer had already left. I asked

Kepala, "How long will it take to get to the location?" He replied. "Four hours… Maybe… boss, call you." I was given an envelope from Kepala. I opened it and it had a card inside with a stamp on it and some printed writing in Indonesian. I asked, "What's this?" He mumbled, "Film permit." I quickly reached into my backpack and placed the permit inside, checking the time. I saw that it was already 11 a.m. It was going to be another busy day.

As we travelled to the next filming location, my phone rang. It was David. "We have a big day planned. I want you to scout the location and determine the price for the stunt team, same as yesterday. Secondly, I want you to film another audition tape for Sarah while you are there. I will email you the details while you're on your journey. Sarah will be waiting for your video tonight. Make this a priority when you get back. Your role depends on it. Thank you for your email last night. It was well received." I replied, "OK, thanks, David. I will contact you later."

Four hours later, we were still stuck in traffic. Kepala seemed to be in a foul mood and traffic was gridlocked. The heat was intense, clinging to every surface inside the tin can. Beads of sweat formed on Kepala's forehead and slowly rolled down his face. My phone battery was getting low as Kepala didn't have a charging point, so I was getting paranoid that no one could contact me. I could see a sea of car roofs stretching endlessly ahead. Traffic had become so congested, that the idea of reaching the destination within a reasonable time frame, seemed like a distant dream. Impatience and irritation continued to seep in. I was stuck in an unfamiliar region and wondered what I was doing there. As the car inched forward, in the standstill traffic, Kepala rolled down his window. Allowing a small breeze to enter the stifling vehicle. Despite the pungent pollution smell hanging in the air, Kepala coughed and spat a big blob of green mucus out of the window. He did my head in! I was exhausted and uneasy, wondering how long until we arrived at our destination. It was as though I was trapped, with no way out. Kepala took two calls and talked in Indonesian. I assumed it was related to the production we were heading for. We stopped at a gas station and while Kepala filled up, I grabbed some food.

When I got back, Kepala was ready to leave and I asked him, "How much longer will it be? He replied, "One hour." I was frustrated. We continued to drive for hours through hills and fields before finally arriving at a dense jungle area, which I presumed was a national park. An armed guard greeted us at the entrance. Kepala spoke with him and passed him some money. The guard wanted to see my permit, which I showed him. He smiled and lifted the barrier, so we could drive into the park. It was clear to me that he had accepted a bribe, despite seeing the permit.

We drove deeper and deeper into the tropical rain forest, until we reached the location. It was so remote; it was the kind of place where you'd get kidnapped and never seen again. We were surrounded by large, ancient trees that towered hundreds of feet. They looked like they were from the Jurassic period. We parked up near a fast-flowing river. It had a massive suspension bridge crossing over it. It looked like the bridge from *First Blood, Rambo*. The sight was like a time warp, transporting us back to a simpler era when nature ruled and people were at their most vulnerable. Kepala said to me, "This is the second location."

There wasn't a soul in sight. The fact that nobody else was there surprised me. It was quite eerie being there alone, with Kepala. It was like being dropped into the middle of nowhere. I felt like I was the only person in the world. Then my phone rang. It was David, he said to me, "I'm glad you're at the location, Byron. What do you think?" I replied, "I can see why you chose this location David, it's just right for kidnapping someone. What a scary remote place." David answered, "Yes, perfect for a kidnapping. In fact, some of the supporters of the Indonesian Islamic state were in that same jungle, but obviously they are not there anymore since the clampdown. I'd like you to audition here. Your character, Gary, will run over the bridge with his kidnapped victim and his team of bandits. A team of ten soldiers will attempt to rescue your kidnap victim and kill some of your guys, but you will escape in the jungle. A French photographer from my company is on his way to the location, where he can help take some stills and film a scene with you, if you wish. He should arrive within an hour. Please give me a full breakdown of how many guys you will need and a price for the stunt team as well. Thankyou"

I replied,"OK, now I understand, David. I was wondering why there wasn't anyone here. I'll wait a bit and look around." He replied, "It's that shitty traffic down there, Byron. He will be with you shortly." The call ended. As I walked around the location, I presumed that the photographer might be the French guy I saw at breakfast. Trying to focus on my audition,

It Ain't All Glitz & Glamour

I went through the script and broke down the scenes for the stunt guys. Meanwhile, Kepala slept in the car. For this action scene, I planned a shootout on the bridge when Gary and his team were being chased with the hostage. During the chase, three of Gary's guys would get shot and fall into the river below. My plan was to set up a wire rig on the bridge for this. As they fall into the ravine below, Gary gets shot in the arm but still evades capture with his victim in tow. They then would escape into the dense jungle. I wanted to add a soldier firing an RPG at Gary for good measure.

As the afternoon passed, I wondered when David's photographer would show up. It was late and the mosquitoes started biting. I realised we only had a few hours of daylight left. I walked back to the car. Kepala was away with the fairies. His head leaned against the door window, his mouth open and he was dribbling. I knocked on the car window. Kepala woke up and looked at me with a bewildered expression on his face. He was alarmed. I said, "Can you find out when the photographer will arrive?" Kepala, wiped the dribble from his mouth and replied, "I call production OK." I walked back over to the suspension bridge, watching the rapids below pound against the rocks. David called me 20 minutes later and said, "Byron, my man, is on his way. He may be an hour late. Please be patient, continue to work until he arrives. He has your number and will call you." I answered, "OK, David, but it is almost 3.30 pm, so he needs to be here sharpish if we want to get this done." David replied, "Ok Byron, I understand. I will call you back."

The exotic jungle lost all its allure after 30 minutes of

exploration. The relentless mosquito bites and profuse sweating, caused by the dense foliage and scorching heat left me restless and frustrated. I began to question how long I could endure this discomfort. Suddenly, my phone rang, shattering the eerie silence of the jungle. It was David. He said, "The French photographer won't make it on time, so he's returning to the hotel due to heavy traffic. There was a crash, so we will have to do this another day. My apologies." Angry, I answered. "He could have called me. We still have hours to drive back!" David replied with a strong tone, "Byron, I understand you must be angry, but I'm doing you a big favour here, please be patient. I'll be on the ground in a few days. I will confront him about this. It's unprofessional. Remember, he is a Frenchman! I will speak with you tonight after you return to the hotel." I replied, "OK, David, please let him know I am not happy about this. I'll talk to you later."

I walked back to the car. As the car's engine was running, it seemed Kepala already knew to return to the hotel. The drive home was another nightmare. There were more cars on the road than I had ever seen before and the traffic never eased. It was exhausting. My phone battery died. We arrived back at the hotel after enduring a gruelling five-hour drive. David called me on Kepala's phone, as soon as we pulled up outside my hotel. Kepala handed me his phone. "Byron, I am facing a huge problem that may jeopardise the entire production, if I don't deal with this. I realise it is late, but I must resolve this issue. The local Indonesian production company on the ground, has warned me that they will cancel the whole operation. For their help with the fixers and company services,

It Ain't All Glitz & Glamour

I wired them some money for the film permits. They have said they haven't received it yet, but my bank reports it was received. My partner and I will be flying to Indonesia with the other producers. They are the main investors in the film, so I need a quick solution, otherwise, we have no movie. After I am on the ground, I can hire a new company. I won't work with them again. I can't fly to Indonesia with my producers and show them nothing. They will lynch me."

I replied, "David, you've put me in a difficult situation. I didn't expect this and it's not my problem. I cannot do that. It's not worth my while anyway, I haven't access to that kind of money." David replied, "I understand what you are saying, Byron. Please listen to me. Indonesian law requires that you get a film permit wherever you go, just like in Thailand. You've lived in Asia for long enough to understand that things are different there. Cash is the only currency! They are like rats compared to me and you. I'll send you six thousand dollars right now, directly to your bank account. You will receive a confirmation link from the Bank of America and a screen shot of the transfer. This is in addition to the two thousand promised. You'll be the man I put in charge of the stunt team, so you can expect a lucrative commission. I am pushing you for the main role. All you have to do is pay for the film permits they gave you, with the money I will send to you right now. Keep the rest as compensation for your time and effort. I will call you back in five minutes." David ended the call.

I pondered for a while. Perhaps he was testing me? He just confirmed he would use my guys for the stunt team. This would change everything. I thought this would be a low-risk opportunity to make a quick profit. I was confident that David would give me the money for the permits right away and that I would have nothing to worry about. David then called me a few minutes later and said, "Thank you for sending me your bank details. I've just sent you six thousand dollars. Your extra two thousand dollars, as promised, will be sent to you at the end of the week. I am sending you the transaction links now. Please check it and I will call you back immediately." I replied, "OK, David, thanks."

I promptly checked the email and the bank transfer details. A hyperlink to the transfer was included in the email. It read, "Byron, as stated, we have sent US$6,000 to your account. Crediting will take 3–4 business days. DIGITAL PASSWORD PROTECTED: 5679013214005." After clicking the link in the email, I was directed to the bank's website, where I entered the 13-digit code. A screen then appeared, confirming the transfer was in progress. Everything was in order when David called me again. "Thank you so much, Byron. The funds are on their way. Please pay the driver for yesterday and today, which is the equivalent of six hundred dollars and send me a copy of the film permits. I'll call you tomorrow morning. Your pick-up time tomorrow is 11 a.m. You will visit some amazing tea plantation sites. Thank you again, Byron. Your help is much appreciated."

There were only a few days left for me to be there and the transfer he sent me would arrive in three days. My plan was to pay Kepala and Banyu in small amounts with my money until the six thousand US dollars were cleared in my bank account. It was my hope that everything would fall into place and I could finally breathe easy. The remainder of David's money would be used to pay them off. I would have four thousand left over. That's not bad for a week's work, plus the extra two thousand would come a week later and I would have landed a film role worth thousands of dollars.

I said to Kepala, "I will go and get the film permit money from the cash machine." He nodded at me. I got out of the car and headed to the ATM opposite the hotel. I put in my pin number and attempted to withdraw the money. The withdrawal was declined. I tried again and it was declined again. On my third attempt, it took my bloody card! I couldn't believe it! Lucky for me, I had another bank card on me. This was the account the money was transferred to. I didn't want to use it in case it was also taken. I remained calm. I returned to my hotel room. I had five hundred dollars in my hotel room safe. I wasn't going to give Kepala all the cash since I needed money for food. I thought two hundred dollars would keep him happy until I could sort out my card. As I walked into the lobby of the hotel, Banyu was waiting with Kepala. I approached them and said, "Sorry guys, I have an issue with my bank. The cash machine took my card and I have no money. I have $200 to give you right now. Kepala didn't look happy when I told him this. I passed them the $200. Banyu mumbled something to him in Indonesian and turned to me. "Is it possible to get the rest of the money tomorrow?" I replied, "Yes." With a forced smile, Banyu replied, "Ok, we'll pick you up tomorrow at 11:00 a.m. See you." Banyu and Kepala walked out of the hotel. Kepala waved his hands in the air like an Italian whose pasta had been cooked badly and cursed me. It was obvious he wasn't happy about not being paid in full. I entered the hotel restaurant and ordered food. I was completely exhausted.

Just as I was about to finish eating, my phone rang. It was David. He breathed heavily and sounded angry. He said,"I just received a call from the Indonesian production saying that you are unable to pay the full amount for the film permits. I sent you six thousand dollars. What's the problem, Byron?" I replied, "David, my ATM card was taken. I put it in the machine and it grabbed it. I will pay them tomorrow, no problem. I have another card available. But before I use that, I need to call my bank, to find out what happened to my card that I lost in the machine. I don't want this one snatched." He answered, "Oh, okay, now I understand. What a relief! You had your card taken, which explains things! Yes, I've heard of this problem in Jakarta. I'll contact Banyu's boss and inform him. If you have any problems, always let me know first before speaking to anyone. You have a busy day tomorrow. I have been in touch with the production team from *The Raid* and one of their advisors will meet you tomorrow. It might be their director of photography who shoots the film. Good night and I'll talk to you tomorrow."

The next day, I contacted Leigh in Thailand and explained the situation. I asked her, if she could send me some money via Western Union. She was working in Hua Hin with her dance team, but she couldn't send it as she had no time. So one of her Thai dancers, Siri said she could help. Siri got one of her friends, Krit, who was a stuntman for the *Ong Bak* live show in Bangkok, to go to Western Union, to transfer the money to me in Jakarta. I really appreciated that gesture, it was a hassle and it was very kind of him to do it. After receiving the Western Union code via email, I met Kepala and Banyu downstairs, in the hotel lobby. From there, we went to the Western Union office to receive the cash.

The Western Union office was directly outside the hotel, so I went there. Banyu stopped me and said, "No good, very bad, we go to another one." It looked fine to me. It was next to a bank and a small office with a guard outside it. The Western Union office had security cameras on both sides of the kiosk and was in a secure area. So I couldn't work out why he said that. So I asked him, "Why?" He replied, "Dishonest." I did not ask any more questions.

He gestured towards his beloved sardine can of a car. After getting into Kepala's car, Banyu got on his motorcycle and followed us. Twenty minutes later, we arrived at the Post Office in the north of Jakarta through the city's congested streets. Banyu was greeted by a security guard, who smiled and shook hands with him. The security guard looked at me up and down and pointed to the Western Union desk. I filled out the Western Union form. After I handed the lady the form, she gave me a massive wad of Indonesian rupiah. I was a millionaire with so many bank notes, that I needed a hand to hold them. Indonesia's currency can make you an instant millionaire. Its highest value note is 100,000 rupiah, which works out to 5 pounds! So for 50 quid, you're a millionaire. It felt good for a moment. As soon as I received the cash, I calculated what I owed Banyu and he gave me a receipt and the film permit for the day. Kepala was passed some cash from

Banyu and Kepala smirked with a greedy smile, just like Gollum from The Lord of the Rings. I emailed David the receipts and told him how much I had paid Banyu and the production company. Once we were all squared up, it was time to travel to the next location.

This was a tea plantation just outside Jakarta. Even Kepala seemed annoyed with all the driving. He was driving so slowly and his constant coughing up of mucus was really getting on my nerves. I tried to be helpful by offering to buy him some medicine, but he refused. I called my acting mate Dave Blazejko, who was filming in India, on WhatsApp to tell him about my nightmare journey and to cheer me up. I said, "Alright Dave, how's it going?" Kepala coughed up another batch of phlegm and spat it out the window. David replied, "Yeah, I am okay. We are filming a movie about when the Brits colonised India. We are doing many scenes involving horses. How's Indonesia and what the fuck is that noise in the background?" I replied, "Well, I've just been driving all over the place mate. To be honest, the traffic is terrible, but I've been to some cool locations. More will happen when the team gets here in 2 days." Kepala cleared his throat and spat a green ball of phlegm out the window again. Dave paused for a moment and answered, "Fuck Yeah, that driver sounds cronk mate. Get them to change drivers." I answered, "Yeah, I will. I felt sorry for him at first, but he seems like he doesn't give a shit. I've been stuck in traffic daily and getting to these locations is a nightmare. Payday will be good, but you see what I have to put up with. Folks back home think it's all glitz and glamour!"

Yet again, Kepala gobbed out the window. David laughed hysterically. I put my phone in video mode and showed Kepala spitting. David said, "People think you get the five-star treatment on these movie sets." I replied, "I will write a book about this one day, mate!" Dave laughed again and Kepala realised I was filming him. As Kepala wiped his lips, he wound up his window. Kepala turned to me and got nasty. He shouted at me, "NO FILMING, NO FILMING!" I replied to Kepala, "Keep your hair on mate, how far is the location?" He replied, "One hour!" As he coughed again, he wound down his window and spat again. I turned the phone back to face me. "Dave, I think he has the hump. He doesn't like being filmed for some reason. I will get back to you later." Dave replied, "Ok, mate, see you later." I ended the call. I put some tissues in my ears and lay on the car's back seat to get some sleep.

Two hours later, I awoke to the deafening sound of rain drops pounding relentlessly on the car roof. Despite having stuffed tissues into my ears, I couldn't escape the incessant noise. We drove up a desolate hill. My boredom reached an intolerable level. Reaching the peak of the mountain, I gazed out at the tea plantations encircling us. We were so high up that clouds engulfed us. Again, we were in the middle of nowhere. Kepala pulled into a parking area, but we couldn't disembark due to the downpour. We were in the midst of a tropical storm, with the rain pouring down in torrents. I sat there, waiting for the deluge to abate. After several hours, it eventually did. Finally, when the rain stopped, we had freedom and got out of the car.

Kepala escorted me to a small wooden shack where a lady cooked chicken. She greeted Kepala with a smile, gave me some BBQ chicken and said to me, "Filming?" I smiled and replied, "Yes." I turned to Kepala and said, "What's going on?" He replied, "We wait here." I ordered water from the chicken lady and my phone rang. It was David. He said, "Hi Byron, I know you are at the location. The production guys will be with you shortly. Please film the action scenes on the mountainside. Price up what we need for the stunt guys. You know what to do." I replied, "The production guys are not here yet and I need help to do some filming." David answered, "I will the call production in Jakarta." I replied, "Ok, David, thank you." I hung up the phone. As I was finishing my chicken, the lady walked past me and said, "No good." I sensed she was referring to Kepala.

I went down to an area overlooking acres and acres of tea plantations. The view was amazing. We were a few hundred feet up. I set up my camera on the hillside. The two wannabe motorcycle guys I had seen in Jakarta turned up and watched me. They waved at Kepala. The strange thing was that they never took off their helmets. They just stood there and stared at me. I called Kepala over to me and said, "You need to help me with the filming." I didn't want to hang around for the other helpers to show up. I needed to make a previs video and explain my idea for the mountain scene, otherwise, I would run out of time and lose the job, if I had nothing to show. Kepala wasn't happy. Again, he didn't want to be filmed. Between takes, he covered his face with a scarf and his hands and turned away. However, with some of the action stuff, I managed to film him in choke holds and me throwing some punches at him. Kepala finally had enough, waving his hands in the air, cursing something in Indonesian and walking back up the hill.

He spoke to the motorcycle guys on his way. It looked like the motorcycle guys were carrying revolvers in the waistband of their jeans. Observing me suspiciously, they all looked at me. After the chicken lady commented on Kepala, it was an awkward situation. For a few minutes, I had bad thoughts. I could get shot up here and no one would bloody know. I started getting paranoid. For a moment, I considered the possibility that I was in danger up there, completely unnoticed. Kepala approached me and began speaking to the bikers in a manner that made me extremely uneasy. I kept my cool. Kepala shouted, "We go back to the hotel." I packed my things and walked over to the car. The motorcycle guys watched me like hawks all the time. We left the tea plantation and returned to Jakarta. Kepala didn't speak to me all the way home. The motorcycle guys followed us behind.

Hours later, we were back at the hotel. That evening, I sent David the previs videos, my risk assessment and ideas for the action scenes. I headed down to the local convenience store outside the hotel to get a coffee. As I came out, I could see Kepala talking to the two motorcycle guys. They stared at me again and I still got bad vibes. I drank my coffee standing outside the store, looking back at them. Shortly afterwards, David called me. He sounded agitated. It was like a thunderstorm in the distance, warning me that something was about to happen, but I couldn't tell what. "Hi, Byron, what's happened at the location? I was contacted by the production and they told me you manhandled the driver and they are considering cancelling the entire project. Despite the fact that I sent you the money, you have been late in paying it. The driver is upset and doesn't want to drive you around." I was amazed by David's spiel. I replied, "I don't know what the driver is on about. All I asked him to do was help me out, with a couple of scenes, as your guys never showed up again! The driver just stood there anyway, when I filmed." David replied with a strong tone. "WELL! You should have waited for my team to arrive. They are professionals. You can't expect the driver to help you!"

I snapped back. "Listen, I've been driving around Indonesia all week like a blue-arsed fly, with that guy Kepala gobbing phlegm out the window. I've spent over 40 hours driving around with that ignorant twat, not speaking to me. Also, not once have the guys turned up as you promised! Only some wannabe biker fools on 125cc motorcycles. You're meant to be the professional organisation! You always had an excuse, so what did you expect me to do? I'm not willing to stand around all day like a Muppet. Quite frankly, I've been doing all the work on the ground here. You're the producer, so sort these problems out!" The conversation was getting tense. It was like a boiling pot, with both of us becoming more and more agitated as the argument escalated. David tried to manipulate the conversation, he tried to take control of it. It was quite strange. His voice suddenly changed into something dark and ominous, just like that demon from the *Evil Dead* movie. It reminded me of when, I've seen lady boys lose the plot fighting with foreigners. He sounded like Satan. I quickly held the phone away from my ear, as he blew his top. It was amusing to me, when he shouted at the top of his lungs. It was like a volcano exploding, spewing out rage and fury in a violent outburst. If you could send fire down the phone, my ears would have burned off! "BYRON! YOU ARE A FUCKING RACIST! YOU DON'T LIKE ASIANS. YOU WOULDN'T HAVE CARED IF THAT HAD BEEN A WHITE MAN IN THE CAR WITH YOU! Who do you think you are talking to? Do you realise who I am? ARE YOU LISTENING TO ME?"

It was as if he had multiple personalities. I could hear him huffing and puffing. He paused for a moment during his hissy fit. Then he shouted, as if talking in tongues, I didn't understand any of it. He displayed a range of emotions that seemed to come from different personalities within him. I could hear him breathing heavily. Then suddenly, he stopped in the middle of his tantrum. Then he started to scream. His voice became louder with each word. Despite my efforts to calm him, he seemed too far gone. He was like a menopausal woman. He needed psychiatric help. He then shouted with a voice like Robert De Niro, "I AM SO TIRED! SO TIRED!" I just looked at my phone, thinking, Jesus, this guy's got some big issues. There was an eerie silence, then I said, "David, listen to me, you need some help!" He exploded again; I opened a big Pandora's Box of split personalities. He shouted a second time down the phone in an angry feminine voice, just like when Helena Bonham Carter played the Red Queen in *Alice in Wonderland*. "SLEEEEEP! Do you realise who I am? I AM

GIVING YOU A LIFE-TIME OPPORTUNITY HERE! I HAVE PUT A LOT OF TIME AND EFFORT INTO THIS PROJECT. I WILL NOT LET IT GO DOWN THE DRAIN, DUE TO YOUR AMATEUR ANTICS AT THE TEA PLANTATION. I HAVE SENT YOU THE MONEY, SO GO DO YOUR JOB! I'VE GOT A GOOD MIND TO CANCEL YOUR BANK TRANSFER RIGHT NOW. IF YOU JEOPARDISE THIS MOVIE, I WILL BLACKLIST YOU FOR LIFE... I can cancel you out! YOU WILL NEVER WORK AGAIN IN THE FILM INDUSTRY AND BE BANISHED TO B MOVIE STARDOM FOR THE REST OF YOUR LIFE!

Waiting for me to answer, he breathed heavily down the phone, just like those weird phone stalkers. I thought then that I didn't want to work with this psycho. I will cut my losses and go home. I wasn't going to argue with him again. I replied calmly. "David. Are you listening?" He didn't reply. But I could hear him breathing heavily. Then I said, "Please blacklist me and see if I care. B movies aren't that bad, I've done enough of them and made a good living from them. As for these idiots you've got down here, they are amateurs and are ripping you off. There are two sides to every story. You know I paid them late because my bank card was taken. I told you that a few days ago, or have you forgotten? As for being a racist, I've lived in Thailand for nearly 20 years and my sister-in-law and my two nieces are Thai, so work that out! Oh and you need medical help!" David shouted with anger and urgency in his voice. He then did a Ronnie Pickering on me! He said, "DO YOU REALISE WHO I AM? Do you realise who I am? Do you realise who I am?" I nearly said Ronnie Pickering! He sounded just like him. Maybe he got the quote from YouTube? I hung up looking at my phone, thinking this guy's not the full ticket. How on earth did he become a movie producer? He reminded me of the stalker Jabba, who harassed me since *Only God Forgives*. There was a lot of similarity between their personalities. If David had been an actor, he could have won an Oscar with that performance.

I started to walk back to the hotel, when I saw Kepala shaking hands with one of the stunt coordinators, I saw at breakfast a few days before. They seemed friendly together. Maybe Kepala was playing games with me, to stop me from getting the job. My phone rang again, it was David. I thought here we go again, this geezers a glutton for punishment, as I'm going to lose my rag in a minute and then for sure, I will never work in the industry again. I answered the call and said, "DAVID NOW... Listen to me! I know you're under a lot of pressure, but I am not willing to be talked to like that by anybody. I don't give a fuck who you are! The Muppets you have on the ground here are quite frankly, a joke! You are unprofessional. I am done. I am flying back to Thailand." David replied, "No! Please don't! Byron, I apologise and I am sorry. I'm under so much stress here. Why? Why? Why?" His voice trembled and he started to cry. At that point, I was thinking we have all heard horror stories about how Hollywood can be pretentious and have lots of drama queens. I presumed this was one of those experiences with him throwing his weight around. I had seen it a couple of times on set with actors, but never with producers. I was surprised at how incapable he was under stress. I turned off my phone.

I started walking up to my hotel entrance. Kepala was standing there smoking with the two motorcycle guys. They knew something was wrong. They watched me as I entered the hotel. In my hotel room, I started to get my things together. I checked the bank transfer on my phone to see if the money was still on the way. It said it was in progress. I thought, well, at least I will get the money from this if nothing else at the end of the week. I logged on to the internet and tried to change my flight ticket. I settled down for the night and watched a movie. I turned my phone on after the film finished and made a cup of tea. There was a call from David, which I picked up. He said, "Hi Byron. I am sincerely sorry; I am under so much stress. This was totally unprofessional of me. I can understand if you are leaving." Usually, David had a loud and boisterous voice, but this time it was different. He seemed more collected and composed, like he was in a better mental space. I replied, "Yes, David, I am leaving." He replied, "That's such a shame." I said, "My flight is booked." I just wanted to get the hell out of there. David then said, "Ok, Byron." I replied, "Bye."

I was so overwhelmed by the unexpected conversation that I needed to process what had just happened. It was weird. My body was tired, so I decided to rest and process the experience the next day. The next morning, I went to breakfast. As I walked by the reception desk, the reception lady said to me, "Mr. Gibson Your room hasn't been paid for yet. When are you checking out?" I replied, "The production will pay for the hotel room and I am not leaving for a couple of days." I made my way to the breakfast area to grab a much-needed coffee and noticed the stunt guy I had seen the night before. He had his rucksack with him and it seemed like he was going location scouting. I couldn't help but think he would finally get the job. I was disappointed that it all fell through. Banyu turned up at the reception and waved at the stunt guy and they left together. After finishing my coffee, I walked around the shopping centre, which was adjacent to my hotel. I was sick and tired of the traffic and I didn't want to walk Jakarta's polluted streets.

Around midday, my phone rang. It was David once again. He was like a stalker. Like a fool, I picked up. He said, "Hi Byron. I am so sorry. I understand that we've had disagreements, but I believe we can work together to resolve them. There are other guys who are pricing up the action scenes, who are staying in your hotel. I have to say that their work doesn't meet our standards. Your contributions, on the other hand, were exceptional and precisely what we needed. Let's talk about how we can move forward and improve our collaboration." I replied, "Well, so far, I have not been confirmed for the job. I've been doing all the dirty work here on the ground and working over 12–15 hours a day, with no rewards. I am leaving unless you confirm me as the man organising the stunt team and military advisors."

David answered, "That's exactly what I called you about. I can confirm you as the guy who will organise the stunt team and military personnel. As for the acting role, you will have to audition with Sarah when we arrive, as there is a procedure we have to follow due to SAG rules. Between me and you, I can confirm you will have that role also. Sarah likes you." I was cautious of David because of his split personality. I didn't want to thank him so much and lick his arse after the way he spoke to me the night before. I know he had just confirmed me, but I was in no mood for more bullshit. I replied to him in a polite but firm way and made it clear that I would not tolerate any further outbursts. I wanted to be sure that the professional relationship between us, would remain intact and that there would be no more unpleasant surprises. I replied, "David. I am very happy you have chosen me. I can guarantee you won't be disappointed." He replied, "I'm glad you are back on board. Take two days off, as I need your full breakdowns and risk assessments for each scene. These assessments should be ready and handed in, when we all arrive in 48 hours' time. This will give you time to learn your lines and get ready for the one-to-one casting. I want you to blow Sarah away. I want to prove a point. After all, I am paying her!" I replied, "Ok, David, thank you. The only thing is that my flight is booked for tomorrow." David answered, "Cancel it. I will get my secretary to book your flight back to Thailand the day after we arrive. I will send you an additional $2,000 after this call for the trouble. We will arrive at 6 p.m. from Los Angeles in the evening. We have a meet and greet booked where you can meet the team." I answered, "Ok, David, thanks." David had another call coming in. I could hear a phone ringing. He said, "I must cut the call short. I have another call. One last thing, can you email me who you recommend for your stunt team and military advisors? I will email you in 10 minutes the details of the next scenes. I will call you back later." I replied, "Ok, not a problem."

It Ain't All Glitz & Glamour

I went back to the hotel and as I walked into the lobby, I could see Kepala and Banyu loitering around outside, with the two motorcycle guys. I ignored them and returned to my room. I proceeded to work on my risk assessments and the action ideas for all the locations I had been to. I checked my email and found that David had sent me the information about the house where Gary would kidnap the lady. He wanted a full breakdown of the action scenes. In another scene near a fish market, he wanted a scene where Gary and his men arrive by boat. I spent the afternoon writing the plan. I also contacted my friend Frank in Marbella about the job.

Working with Frank gave me great confidence to execute my plan properly, as he had a wealth of knowledge of firearms and warfare. I also felt that the stunt team I had put together was highly capable and could deliver the action David was looking for. Later that evening, David called me back. He said, "Byron, do you have all the information ready for the assessments?" I replied, "Yes, David. I will send them over shortly." David answered, "Ok, Byron. I knew I could count on you. Now, who are you recommending for the military team?" I replied, "I have a friend in Marbella called Frank. He's 100 percent solid and he's a guy you can trust. He's worked on many movie sets with me. He's your man." David spoke in an upbeat tone. "That's brilliant. I would appreciate it if you could send me his profile and contact information."

I replied, "Yes, I've spoken to him already and he knows about the job." David replied, "You should get a management job! Which other guys do you recommend for the stunt team?" I replied, "Well, I have some friends in Bangkok who are in the stunt industry." David's tone changed into a disapproving one. He said, "I appreciate your input. Please avoid actors, military personnel, or stunt performers from there. It's imperative that my production work with someone who meets my standards. I have done business with many of the Europeans from there and I wasn't impressed." I was baffled and asked, "Why is that, David? He replied, "I've had two dealings with some French stunt coordinators from Bangkok and I wasn't pleased with their performance. I had one American coordinator from there who did a bad job too. I know 90 percent of them. I have had some Canadians and Koreans over and don't want to work with any of them. I cannot disclose any further information because that would be against my business practice."

I wanted to keep the deal on track and didn't intend to jeopardise all the arduous work I had put in. So I asked no more questions. Judging by his strong tone, he was adamant that he didn't want anyone from there. I replied, "Okay, I understand. I can get a team from the UK or some from China or Hong Kong." David replied, "I have had some guys work for me from the UK who were great, so yes. As for China and Hong Kong, I do not want to use them. I've been there and done that!" I left it there, as I could tell he wasn't impressed by whoever he had met from that neck of the woods as well. It made me curious who it was, though.

I replied. "Ok David. I will get a stunt team sorted out for you by the time you arrive." He replied, "Ok, Byron, thank you. Do you mind travelling to two locations for me tomorrow? It won't take long. I will need a previs video and a

It Ain't All Glitz & Glamour

breakdown of the action scenes we need to shoot." I answered, "No, that's not a problem. What time will they pick me up?" "Your pick-up is at 8 a.m. so you will have an early start. I will send you the details after this call. Oh and tomorrow Sarah would like to talk with you. Is that OK?" I replied, "Ok, David, that's not a problem and yes, Sarah can call me. I look forward to it." David answered, "See you tomorrow evening. After all this, I am looking forward to finally meeting you. Good luck with the call from Sarah. See you soon." David hung up the phone.

David emailed me shortly thereafter about the scenes he wanted previs videos and breakdowns for. The first breakdown was taken from a scene in the film where Gary and his men arrive by boat at a fishing port in Jakarta's bay under darkness. The location needed to be scouted. The second scene shows Gary kidnapping his hostage from a house in Jakarta. The bandits abduct her and take her to the jungle. David wanted the breakdown to be comprehensive, so he requested a video that detailed the scouting of the location and the movements of the characters in the scene. He also requested a breakdown of the kidnapping scene, which would include an overview of the house and the jungle. It took me most of the evening to come up with some cool scene ideas. After contacting Frank, I told him I would put him in charge of the military team. I outlined my ideas in detail over the phone and told him I was waiting for David's confirmation. Then I would hand the full operation over to Frank and let the professionals handle it. I had spent several hours brainstorming and outlining my ideas and I was exhausted. I decided to take a break and get some sleep. The next morning, I awoke bright and early. I was ready for Sarah's call. I made myself a coffee and then my phone rang. It was from a number I didn't recognise. I presumed it was Sarah.

I answered the call, "Hello, Byron, speaking." A lady with a Californian accent replied, "Hi, Byron its Sarah. I am pleased to speak with you." I replied, "Yes I am pleased to speak with you too Sarah." She replied, "We have limited time for the casting. I will arrive a day after David. The role you are casting for is critical to the project's success, it requires someone with the right skills, experience and look. I'm looking forward to learning about your journey and tapping into your expertise. David and I have worked together on this project for a while now. He has told me a lot about you and your work. I'm excited to work with you and see what creative ideas you have for this casting, my darling." I replied to Sarah, "Likewise, Sarah, I am really looking forward to it." Sarah continued to say, "Since the casting process can be quite tricky and requires a lot of preparation, it is imperative to have someone who can fluently read through the script beforehand, in order to ensure that the process runs smoothly. Reading up to six pages of the script, will give me a better understanding of the characters and their motivations. As a result, I will be able to make the appropriate decisions regarding the project. You also have to be physically up for it. Are you happy with that?"

I replied, "Yes, I am Sarah. It's not a problem." She replied enthusiastically. "That's awesome. You are such an awesome guy to speak to!" I answered, "I'm always happy to help out Sarah." She said, "Do you have a partner, Byron?" I replied, confused. "Yes, I do, Sarah. Why?" She replied, "Wow, she must be so lucky to have a real man. Most of the hunky men in the film industry are gay! Leaving us ravenous women high and dry!" I didn't like where the conversation was heading. I thought she was trying to do a Harvey Weinstein on me. Sarah went on to say, "Would you mind casting with your shirt off?"

Her language suggested her intentions were not pure. I felt like she was asking too much of me and that I didn't have to resort to such lengths to accurately portray the character. I wanted to make sure that she understood that I wasn't comfortable with the suggestion and wanted to be respected. I replied, "Sarah, I'm an actor, I'm not into that kind of thing!" Straight away, she said sarcastically, "Well, most actors I know will take it in every orifice to get the job!" I laughed at this point, I had to put my hand over my mouth. I wondered if she was playing me to see my reaction.

She said, "Have I offended you? I am sorry, I get carried away sometimes being the hot milf I am. I understand you are uncomfortable with what I said. I am sorry. It won't happen again. I am a rotten girl!" Her voice was low and sincere. Now I thought, bloody hell, I'm in a freak show. Besides crazy David with a psychotic personality, I have to deal with a sexual casting director who wanted phone sex! I was taken aback by her sudden change in behaviour and couldn't help but feel uneasy. After all, she had just shifted from flirtatious to being apologetic in a blink of an eye. Her apology seemed genuine and I appreciated it, but I was still on edge. It was almost like she had two different personalities. This made the situation even more confusing and difficult to know how to proceed.

After a moment, I replied to her, "It's OK, Sarah, I've not taken it to heart." She replied, "That's OK, honey. I will see you in a few days. I am a patient milf." I replied, "See you soon." I was dumbfounded. I had heard of the casting couch process in the film industry. I knew of some actors, who engaged in it, both male and female. Some work in Hollywood today. I always remember working on an Indian movie on a massive boat and the Ukrainian and Belarusian models, were shagging the Indian stars, on the deck below to get parts. I never thought anyone would try it on me. I headed off to breakfast to collect my thoughts and try to make sense of what had just happened.

After breakfast, Kepala and Banyu picked me up at 8 a.m. Banyu gave me two more permits for both locations and I paid him for them. By 9a.m I was on my way to the house where Gary was going to kidnap his victim. Another hot and humid day greeted us. Our journey to the location was filled with Kepala coughing as usual and sulking. I was happy that all of this would soon be over. Thus, I would no longer have to drive around with this uncouth Muppet. We were meandering along a central Jakarta Street when a policeman on a motorcycle came up behind us and flashed his lights. He pulled us over. As the policeman walked beside our vehicle, Kepala rolled down the window. The policeman smiled and looked at me in the back of the car. They started talking in Indonesian. It looked like they were talking about me. Clearly, they were familiar with each other. During their conversation, Kepala took out his wallet and paid the policeman a wad of dirty notes. The policeman swiftly put the notes away and smiled at Kepala, patting him on the shoulder. He then hopped back on the bike. Kepala watched him in his rear-view mirror. After getting on his bike, the copper drove away. Meanwhile, Kepala turned to me and said, "Police, my friend." As if to say, don't fuck with me!

Within twenty minutes, I was at the house where Gary planned to kidnap his victim. An antique Dutch colonial house served as the location. An enormous black steel fence surrounded the property. As I approached the gates, Kepala urged me to wait. There was no one to greet us at the house because it was locked. Meanwhile, Kepala made a phone call. After taking notes at the location, I started thinking about what could be shot from the outside. 30 minutes later, a caretaker showed up. We were unable to enter the location after Kepala talked to him for a while. It looked like they were disagreeing. We couldn't go inside, Kepala said, "We'll come back later. We go to the second location."

The second location was a fish market in Jakarta's bay. It was a dirty and messy slum area. It was a chaotic place, with lots of small, colourful fishing boats bobbing up and down in the dark polluted waters. Fishermen were tending to their catch and sorting out their nets. There was a stench coming from decaying fish carcasses left to rot on the pier by some fishermen. I walked around the narrow, maze-like alleys to get ideas for the film. I took a turn and walked through what seemed to be a blizzard of buzzing black flies. The pungent smell of the fish was overwhelming. Around a dozen men, women and children huddled around piles of black mussels, sorting the good ones from the bad and separating the meat from the shell. Discarded mussel shells crunched under my feet as I navigated another alley. I had to turn sideways to squeeze between people standing outside fish stalls and tin-roofed shacks.

I started recording a video of my idea for this scene when Gary came ashore with his team. I took a few notes and didn't want to stay too long, as I felt uneasy there. A few of the locals gave me evil stares. I was the only white guy there. This was strictly not a tourist area. I was alone and all I had was Kepala in the car. I got done as quickly as possible, returned back to the car and told Kepala to go to the hotel.

I settled down for lunch in my hotel room. I had ordered room service to be delivered, so I laid out the food on the bed and sat down to eat. It was a peaceful and relaxing atmosphere and I enjoyed my lunch leisurely. Meanwhile, in Thailand, Leigh was with her dancers in Hua Hin. She hadn't slept much the night before, so she went downstairs and sat outside the hotel. She had a weird feeling about the film. She decided to Google films in Indonesia to see whether she could find anything online. There wasn't much on there. However, within the search engine, it came up with a couple of blogs on a film scam happening in Jakarta.

She read the blogs thoroughly and the more she read, the more she became convinced that I was on the same scam in Jakarta. She decided to take extra precautions and research more thoroughly before calling me. She did more research and it sounded just like what I had been sucked into, where everything was laid out so well. Permits for locations were required. She couldn't believe her eyes. It was like pieces of a

It Ain't All Glitz & Glamour

puzzle coming together, with each piece providing more and more evidence, until the full picture was complete and she was certain I was on the same scam. This confirmed her suspicions, which prompted her to call me in Jakarta.

I had just finished my coffee and Leigh called. She said, "Hi darling, make sure you're in a safe place. I've got something terrible to tell you." I was confused. I wondered what it was. I asked, "I am in my room. What's wrong?" She answered, "The film you are on is a scam! They've been doing it for some time. It's on Google, I'm so sorry." I said, "What? What do you mean?" Leigh replied, "It's a major film scam. They've been enticing people down there for years, extorting money from all kinds of people in the industry. It's huge. This job sounds exactly like the one you are currently working on. Please be careful. Give me a minute, I will send you the links." I couldn't believe what I heard. The links appeared on my WhatsApp and I scoured them carefully.

My heart sank when I knew immediately that this was the same scam. I was left completely speechless, unable to comprehend the magnitude of what had just happened. I called Leigh back immediately and said, "Hi darling, you are right! SHIT! I am so sorry about this. I can't believe I didn't see it!" Leigh replied, "Get the hell out of there and get to the airport!" I replied, "I will. I don't think I will have time to book a flight. I've got to escape here and I don't want them to see me. Can you book me the first flight out tonight, please? Leigh said in a worried tone, "Sure, send me your passport details and ring me when you're on the way. Are you sure you'll be, OK?" I answered, "Don't worry, darling, I will be safe. I will ensure that! I will call you back shortly. I've got to pack." Leigh replied, "Ok, darling, don't do anything stupid! Stay safe. I love you!"

Upon learning that I had been sucked into a major international scam, I was in a state of shock. How fucking stupid was I? I felt embarrassed and foolish, for putting myself in such a vulnerable position. I was thinking about the alleged payday and another role in an action film. The anger I felt towards myself was overwhelming. Not only had I let myself down, but also Leigh. I was so angry. From the window of my apartment, I stared into the distance, trying to make sense of it all. I was filled with despair, feeling like my own foolishness had cost me dearly. I realised Frank was leaving for Malaysia.

I quickly called him. It was 6 a.m. in Spain. He picked up. I said, "Frank, I've got a problem. This movie is a total scam. I'm sorry mate. Whatever you do, don't go to Malaysia. I am about to do a runner. Frank asked, "What do you mean it's a scam?" I replied, "Leigh just called me. She found out it's a scam and saw it on Google! It's some Indonesian mafia scam extorting money by setting up fake castings and fake movie sets. They've conned thousands of people. They call this person who conned me, The Con Queen of Hollywood." Frank calmly replied, "Stay where you are. I will call you back. It's early here and I don't want to wake the kids."

When I put down the phone, my thoughts turned to anger and extreme paranoia. I paced around the room like a madman. I tossed things around and kicked the bin. "FUCK! FUCK! FUCK!" I shouted. What a fool I was! I marched out of my apartment and into the hallway, kicking the wall and wanting to kill them. A couple passed me on their way to their room. They looked at me in fear. I strutted down the corridor like a rabid maniac towards the lift. I passed some cleaners who looked at me and fled into the apartment they were cleaning. They quickly bolted the door. In a deep state of rage, I headed to reception to confront the low-life bastards who had done this to me.

When I got to the lift, I pressed the down button. The lift doors opened. There was a couple with a young child and they sensed something was wrong. When the young boy started crying, I regained my senses. I was consumed by anger. In that moment, the child's tears reminded me of the consequences of my actions. It was enough to make me take a step back and breathe deeply. Walking backwards out of the lift, I said, "I am sorry." After they pressed the button to go down, the lift door closed. I had to devise a plan. I strutted back to my room. I was still infected by the devil. The devil spoke to me and laughed at me to open the gates of hell. I thought my life was in danger. What was all this bullshit about? The motorcycle guys were there for Kepala's and Banyu's protection, I assumed. They looked like twats, but any twat could shoot you with a gun! I was overwhelmed by the situation and my heart raced as I tried to understand what was going on. I sat on the bed, thinking about revenge. What would I do? How would I escape? Are there more of them? Do they have weapons? They must have been well connected to organise such an operation. It seemed to me that everyone was on the take. Everybody who stopped us on our journey, from security guards to policemen, seemed to be getting bribed.

Eventually, I focused and came up with a plan. The predators would become the prey! I'm not the poncy actor they think I am! I was determined not to let these scammers take advantage of me. I was determined to fight back and not be a victim. I took a deep breath and assessed the situation. I thought about what resources I had available to me and how I could use them to my advantage. I was ready to use all of my skills and knowledge to take control of the situation.

My plan was to head down to the lobby and invite Kepala and Banyu to my room for a coffee. Once in my room, I would knock them out and hold them captive. I would hold them both captive in the shower. Once I had the bastards where I wanted them, I was going to call the Con Queen, who was impersonating David Ready and demand all my money back and a ransom. Or both of my hostages would get beaten. I figured this would be the quickest way to get back my money and take back control of the situation.

It was an extreme plan, but I had to take matters into my own hands since the police were unable to help me. If that didn't work, I would seize all their money, cell phones and cash cards and force them to give me their pin numbers. I was going to take their car and motorcycle keys and both their IDs. To top it off, I would strip them both naked and tie them together as if they were in a doggy-style position, bumming each other around the base of the toilet. I was going to bin their clothes on my way out. My plan was designed to humiliate and embarrass them, as well as ensure that they would be unable to pursue me. By taking their car and motorcycle keys, they could not chase me. By stealing their

It Ain't All Glitz & Glamour

IDs, they could not report the incident and if something happened to me, I would have their IDs. By stripping them naked and tying them together, they would be too embarrassed to make a scene. All of this would give me enough time to get away and be safe before they were found. Then I would get out of Jakarta. They wouldn't find them till the next day, when the cleaners came in and I would be long gone.

I started to get to work. I knew that Kepala and Banyu couldn't carry weapons into the hotel as the detector would go off at the entrance. I presumed they would be clean. I honestly thought the motorcycle guys were packing revolvers and they were always outside, so things were in my favour. Nevertheless, I didn't want to take any chances. At this point, I feared for my life. I knew I needed to be very tactical in my planning. As I walked down the hall, I saw a fire point near the lift. I opened the glass panel and took the red axe back to my room. With the red axe in hand, I knew I could defend myself if necessary. I wanted to make sure I had something I could use to protect myself in case they attacked me. The red axe was the perfect tool! I felt more confident and ready to face any danger if it presented itself. I rushed back to the fire point and got a fire extinguisher to spray in their faces for added measure.

The cleaners left their cleaning trolley a few doors down. I quickly sneaked out and took two bottles of bleach and all their sugar. I slipped back into my room. I unscrewed the bleach bottle lids and placed bleach in the shower. I knew that bleach would temporarily blind them if sprayed in their eyes. I also wanted something to throw that was hot enough to be a deterrent. So, I boiled the kettle and put sugar in it. I would throw that in their faces, a bit of icing on the cake! The curtains had drawstrings, so I cut the strings off with a cutlery knife and knotted them together to make a rope. I also ripped up my duvet cover and turned it into long strips to tie the fuckers up with. I took out the pillows from the pillowcases and put them in the bathroom to put over their heads. I cut the cable from both the hair dryer and TV and stripped it down so the wire was exposed, so I could electrocute them. I was sure I could take them by surprise and come out victorious, as I had prepared in advance. By having my weapons around the door entrance, I knew I could reach for them quickly if things got out of hand.

The odds seemed to be in my favour with all this ready to roll in my forthcoming battle for justice. I felt confident I could take them easily. They wouldn't expect that shit. After everything was all set up, I made my way confidently downstairs. Banyu and Kepala were waiting at the hotel's front entrance, talking to the motorcycle guys. After walking to the lobby, I saw the French photographer leaving through the front door. I knew that if I confronted the photographer, my actions would put me in danger. Banyu and Kepala were already suspicious and likely to act if I said anything. Furthermore, the motorcycle guys outside watched me.

This meant that if I did anything to alert the photographer, they would be ready to intervene. Banyu sensed something was wrong and asked, "Is there a problem?" My phone started to ring. I turned my back on Kepala. It was Frank calling. I quickly answered and Frank said, "What's the situation?" I replied, "Just a moment." I walked to the hotel lift and left Banyu and Kepala standing in bewilderment.

I said to Frank, "I will hold the fuckers to ransom. I will bring them up to my room, knock them both out and demand my money back from the Con Queen. The room is primed and ready to go." Frank replied. "What the fuck are you doing? It's time to get the fuck out of there. Call the British Embassy. If you do anything to those scumbags, you are going to spend alot of time in some shitty prison and it will work in their favour. Remember where you are? You are in Indonesia! They are the mafia and connected to all kinds of people. It's not going to end well, Byron. You don't want to end up in jail! You could serve a life sentence for kidnapping and extortion. Get your fucking shit together and leave as soon as you can. Shave your beard, stay in public places and make sure they aren't following you!" I replied, "I will call you back."

I paused for a few minutes. I was thinking about what Frank had said to me. The phone call brought me back to my senses. What was I thinking? I calmly walked back to Kepala and Banyu. I would have loved to have launched a roundhouse kick at Kepala's head at that point. However, I was surrounded by customers in the hotel. I remained calm and said, "I've been fighting with my wife. Give me an hour and I will be ready to go to the film location." Kepala wasn't impressed. Banyu said, "Ok, one hour." They both grudgingly nodded and left. I stopped walking back to the lift and suddenly thought, wait a minute, has the hotel room been paid for? I shouted to them, "Hold on, Banyu! Come back!" Stopping them both in their tracks. I waved them over and proceeded to the reception.

I turned to the receptionist and asked, "Has my hotel room been paid for?" She checked her computer, surprised. "No, your room hasn't been paid yet." I felt like slamming their faces down on the reception desk. I pointed to Kepala and Banyu and asked them, "Why hasn't my hotel room been paid for? You need to pay for my room now!" They both looked angry and the receptionist smiled in an uneasy manner. Banyu pulled out a wad of notes and put them on the desk. I thought that the receptionist might be in on the scam, as she had been overly friendly with these guys in the past. So, to protect myself, I got a receipt for the payment. This was to ensure that I wouldn't be falsely accused of not paying the hotel bill when I tried to leave the country. I then said to Kepala and Banyu, "Ok guys, I will see you in one hour."

They left pretty pissed off and walked through the body scanners and out of the hotel. I watched as they complained to the two motorcycle guys outside. I returned my room. I started to gather my essential belongings. I knew the receptionist might alert Banyu and Kepala if I escaped with my suitcase. I had to be discreet and pack a small Adidas backpack. I packed what I could in the backpack and left the rest of my clothes in the hotel. I couldn't shave my beard as I had no razor! The axe, the fire extinguisher, the ripped-up bed sheets, curtain strings, bleach and electric cables were all still where I placed them for the trap. When I closed the hotel room door, I laughed at myself as I thought whoever makes a cup of tea with that kettle will find it bloody sweet! Plus, the cleaners will wonder who that nutter was who stayed in that room. I proceeded downstairs. As I passed the reception area,

I smiled at the receptionist and said, "I'm just off to get a cup of coffee and will return in an hour. Have my guys wait here if you see them." While picking up her phone, the receptionist eyeballed me leaving. I walked out of the reception area and through the lobby.

I could see my driver and his assistant and the motorcycle guys outside, having a cigarette with their backs to the hotel doors. I couldn't leave there. I immediately entered the fire escape room. I carefully opened the door and crept down the staircase, making sure to stay out of sight. I was lucky that on the third floor there was an open door leading to a restaurant. I went inside. I didn't know where I was headed. I walked through the kitchen, where some chefs cooked noodles. A big, fat chef looked at me, wondering if I was some kind of madman running around in his kitchen. He shouted something at me in Indonesian. There were plenty of woks, pots and pans in that kitchen and in the mood, I was in, I would have turned him into Chow Mein if he stopped me.

I walked so fast and was determined that no one would challenge me. I made it to the front of the restaurant and the waitresses and chefs stared in shock. I jumped over the counter and was on the third floor of a shopping mall. As I weaved through shoppers, I looked around to see if any scammers were following me. I rushed to the taxi rank. I saw a woman exiting a cab. I jumped into the car as soon as she got out of the back seat! She thought I was an impatient and rude westerner. The taxi driver looked at me like I was a nutcase. I slammed the door shut and told the driver, "Airport, I will give you $50!" He replied, "OK!" The driver pulled away and we started to leave the shopping mall taxi rank.

We came to the main street. It was chockablock with traffic. I looked out the window and saw Kepala and Banyu still waiting outside and looking in my direction. I ducked down. Then my phone rang. It was the Con Queen impersonating David. He said, "Byron, where are you? Is everything alright? The fixers told me you needed an hour off. I have locations and staff waiting for you." I didn't want my cover blown. I said, "I am arguing with my wife. I just want to remind you that my hotel wasn't paid for." The Con Queen replied, "We were going to pay that at the end of your trip. Byron, I can tell you're stressed. Relax for the next hour and then go to the next location with the fixers this afternoon. I will see you tonight." I replied, "Ok, David, see you tonight. By the way, where are you?" I knew he was meant to be flying at this point. He said, "I am in the Silverkris lounge at Changi Airport Singapore right now, having a wine with the team." He hung up.

As the traffic started to move, I got up and looked behind me to see if I was being followed. The two motorcycle guys drove my way. Maybe they spotted me? The taxi driver at this point looked like he wondered what the hell was going on with me bobbing up and down in the back. My phone rang shortly afterwards, it was Leigh. "Hi, darling, where are you?" I quickly answered, "I am on the way to the airport. I don't think it's that far." Leigh stuttered, "You are safe though, right?" I answered calmly, as I knew she was scared, "Yeah, I am safe and any luck with booking the flight tickets?" Leigh replied, "No, not yet, but I am trying. Most of them are booked up." I looked out the back window. The two motorcycle guys were still following me.

I replied to Leigh, "Darling, let me get to the airport, then we can sort it out from there. I've only got 4 percent battery life on my phone." She replied, "Ok, darling, try and get it charged as soon as possible. Call me when you arrive at the airport." I then asked the taxi driver, "Can we take the Tollway?" The taxi driver said, "Yes, very good." The reason I said that was because I knew motorcycles weren't allowed on tollways. At this point, my phone beeped, telling me to charge the phone. However, the problem I had, was that I left the charger in the hotel room and the taxi driver didn't have a phone charger either. The phone was down to 3 percent and then it rang again. It was Frank. "Byron, where are you?" I replied, "I am safe. On the way to the airport, I am nearly there, my battery's going on my phone. I have to hang up, Frank. I will call you back."

I immediately called the British Embassy. A receptionist answered my call. She said, "Hi, The British Consulate Jakarta, how can I help you?" I replied, "Hi, I am a British citizen and I have been involved in a major international film scam in Jakarta." The receptionist replied concerned, "Are you safe? Film scam? Can you tell me more, please?" I replied, "I have very little time as my battery is running out on my phone. Can you give me any advice on what I should do?" The receptionist replied, "You will need to report this to the police in Jakarta and to us." I wasn't willing to do that, as the police were on the take. My phone was beeping, signaling that the battery was dying. I quickly replied, "I can't do that." My phone went dead.

I was relieved when my taxi pulled up at the airport a few minutes later. I paid the taxi driver and thanked him. As I got out of the taxi, I had all these thoughts. Maybe the people who conned me had guys at the airport? Are the motorcycle guys waiting for me there? I was dropped off in the public parking lot that runs parallel to the airport, a few minutes from the main entrance. One thing I noticed when I was dropped off was that the car parking area had no security cameras. This was the same place the scammers had picked me up from.

As soon as I saw the security cameras outside the airport's shops and cafes, I bolted for them. If something happened, I would at least have some protection because I would be in a public area. If anyone approached me, I was ready to defend myself with my fists clenched. The airport's main entrance had a security guard stationed at the doors. I knew I would be safe here, or at least I hoped so. After entering the airport's main hall, I paced around looking for a phone charging point but couldn't find any. Five minutes after scouting the area, I noticed a bag wrapping service and a guy sitting down at the desk, staring at his phone plugged into a charger.

I approached the guy, I politely asked if I could plug my phone into his charger for ten minutes. He gladly obliged.

I sat next to the plastic wrapping machine. I leaned against the wall. I looked around for suspicious characters. Ten minutes passed, I took my phone back from the nice guy at the wrapping service and gave him $5. When I turned my phone on, it had 25% battery life, enough to book my flight. My first thought was to call Leigh.

It Ain't All Glitz & Glamour

She picked up immediately and said, "I was worried. Where are you? Are you safe?" I replied, "I am at the airport and yes, I am safe." Leigh replied, "I am still searching for a flight. There's one at 7.10 p.m. which I am trying to book right now." I have to hang up and call you back to book it." I replied, "Ok, thanks, darling, get on it. I will wait for your call." I hung up. I heard my phone ring again and it was the Con Queen. After 20 rings, it stopped. Within a split second, Leigh called me back. "Your flight is booked, you're flying with Lion Air. It's time to come home, baby. I will send you the details via WhatsApp now." I replied, "Thank you so much, darling." She answered in an emotional tone, crying. I have to finish the show with the girls now. I can't wait to see you." I replied, "I don't know what I would do without you. I can't wait to see you again. I love you so much. Let me go now. I'm almost home and dry and nothing can go wrong. In a few hours, I'll call you. I love you, sweetheart." Leigh replied, "I love you too."

The time was 4.10 p.m. The check-in desks were in sight. I saw several Indonesian guys walking towards me and they stared at me. Did these guys belong to the same gang that had scammed me? We eyed each other up, as we approached each other. I knew I needed to be near people, so I moved next to a couple. I glanced back at the guys as they pushed past me. They continued walking while looking back at me. The Lion Air desk was in front of me. Immediately, I made my way to it. I checked in, showing the hostess my passport and ticket details. While the group of Indonesian guys watched me. The hostess asked, "Do you have luggage?" I replied, "No, just my rucksack." As soon as I checked in, I went to passport control. After turning to look back, I saw the two motorcycle guys staring at me, from the airport doors.

Once I passed passport control, I knew I was safe. I would be out of the main public area and in a secure space. Passport in hand, I walked up to the immigration officer. When he looked at my passport, he said, "You have many passport stamps?" I replied, "Yes, I am an actor. Is there something wrong?" He pondered and slowly looked through my passport and occasionally looked at his computer. There was a sense of anxiety in me. Maybe these people had planted drugs in my hotel room. The immigration officer quickly stamped my passport and returned it to me, much to my relief! The transit lounge gave me a happy feeling as I walked through it. Wanting to leave Indonesia, I went to the departure gate. I sat down in a corner and relaxed.

Approximately an hour and a half remained before my flight took off. I called Frank, he picked up straight away. I said, "Frank. I am at the airport and I've got a flight back." Frank replied, "Great work! Keep a low profile. Call me when you're in Bangkok and have a safe trip." I replied, "No worries, I'll talk to you soon." Just as I was boarding, my phone started ringing. It was the Con Queen. I looked at the phone and never answered it. It rang about 20 times, then stopped. A message came up on my phone from him saying, "Please call me back ASAP."

The flight wasn't full and I had three chairs to myself. I stretched out on them. At this point, I was mentally exhausted. I took a selfie of myself and sent Leigh a message to say I was safely on the flight. I had just finished the message and then my phone rang yet again and it was the parasite, the Con Queen. I turned the phone off and thought, fuck him. The plane taxied down the runway and I fell asleep. Four hours later, I woke up and my flight landed in Bangkok. When I arrived home, I was greeted by our two cats, which I picked up and cuddled. I sent Leigh a voice message to inform her that I had arrived home safely. I contacted Frank to let him know that I was home.

My phone began to ring. It was the Con Queen again. I let it ring, then it stopped. After a minute, it started again and rang again about twenty times. Then it stopped and started ringing again. I picked up the phone. The Con Queen said, "Byron, this is David, where the hell are you? My guys came back to pick you up and you weren't there? Please, can you explain to me why you weren't there?" I said to him, "I wasn't there, you CUNT! Because I was flying back to Thailand!" He then said in a shocked voice. "It's not acceptable for you to talk to me like that! What are you doing back in Bangkok? You are meant to meet me tonight!" I answered back, "Let's cut the bullshit. I want to congratulate you on a very compelling con. I admit that you had me, for a few days. You're a superb actor. You could win a Grammy. Well, done! You did your research, which must have taken you months. You are excellent at what you do. You covered all the bases. I don't know where you got the information about me, to lure me in like that. However, you did it very well and you were spot on! You're a low-life scumbag who feeds off people's dreams. If I ever see you, you will be fucked. I promise you that!"

David sneered, "Oh, is that right? You can't touch me! I know everything about you! I have your passport details and your home address. I know where your family are! You don't even know where I am, you fool! I am going to send some guys around to your place tonight and take you out." I replied, "Bring it on, motherfucker! Now fuck off!" He replied as if he were the Greek god, Narcissus. "I WILL FUCK YOU UP! I WILL FUCK YOU UP! Do you realise who I am?" I replied, "You are a fucked-up debauched parasite!" I hung up the phone and there was no point in talking to this bloodsucker anymore.

I needed to get things sorted. I checked my bank account details to see if any funds had been withdrawn, thankfully, they hadn't. I called the bank and told them about my situation. They froze my account. I fired up my laptop and started to go through the emails from David, like a man possessed. I blocked all emails from him and blocked his calls. I changed all passwords and did security checks. I checked the Bank of America bank transfer that David had sent me. It couldn't be opened by my laptop and it came up with the notice that it contained a virus. I started to worry about my own personal security. I had a chainsaw in a cupboard that we had used on a movie set. I put that near my front door, just in case someone kicked it down, so I could do a Scarface on them. I had a high-powered crossbow, a 3-foot machete and two 2000 bolt Tasers on hand, which were all used on film sets. I also had some knives and placed them next to me on the sofa.

It Ain't All Glitz & Glamour

I checked downstairs to see that the security doors were locked and then returned to my apartment. I checked from my balcony and checked that the security guard was on duty outside our condo. Eventually, I fell asleep on the sofa. At 5a.m. I woke up. Straight away, I began to analyse what had happened in Indonesia. I wondered if I suffered from psychosis. Had I been suffering from this for some time? I sat there for hours, judging myself. I pulled myself together. My mind wasn't going to play tricks on me. I wanted to find out why I was a target and so vulnerable.

So guys, this is how I became a victim of one of the biggest and most complex film scams to ever strike the entertainment industry. My transformation into Sherlock Holmes began the next morning. In this con, David Ready and Sarah Finn were impersonated by a clever individual known as the Con Queen of Hollywood. The Con Queen was able to gain the trust of his victims by using information he had gathered about Sarah and David. This allowed him to authentically replicate their mannerisms and personalities. He also had a great understanding of their backgrounds and used that knowledge to create a believable persona. By switching between these two personas, the Con Queen gained the trust of his victims and was able to pull off the scam successfully with his goons in Indonesia. My research led me to discover a way to track a person's IP address from an email. The Con Queen had emailed me with two different emails.

One of the emails came from ready.david@outlook.com and the other was from Sarah@sarahfinncasting.com. The Con Queen made a bogus website and fake email for Sarah

Finn Casting. He had registered the film project on IMDB and everything was in place for his sting. He had a script and covered his back in every way while researching me and my acquaintances in the industry. However, I was able to track both IP addresses due to one mistake he made. The process was easier than I expected. What happened next shocked me. The Sarah Finn website was registered in Los Angeles and the email seemed to come from there. But the David Ready email was a game-changer. I located him. He got sloppy there. To my disbelief, it was an IP address in Lancashire, Manchester, UK. It even pointed to the hotel he was at. To be honest with you, I didn't believe it. I thought it was too good to be true. I checked again and again and it came up with the same location.

I searched on Google maps and it came up with the hotel. I screen shot it and noted where it was. My first thought was that this was bullshit and the impersonator used some sort of proxy service to hide their IP addresses to divert it to Manchester. I didn't believe this scammer was from the UK! My phone had logged the Con Queens phone numbers and I found a website that allowed me to track the numbers. The phone on which he called me was supposedly located in California, which contradicted his IP address, so this confused me. Later, I found out that your cellular phone number can be changed through a proxy diverter available online. At this point, I didn't know where the Con Queen was.

I started to note down, certain things he said to me during my time in Jakarta. It took me a while to figure out how the Con Queen knew so much about me. However, it dawned on me that the majority of the information must have come from people I knew in the film industry. The Con Queen mentioned, he didn't want to use any of the guys from Bangkok or China. I presumed, some of them had spent time there and been ripped off. While I was in Jakarta, I had several conversations with the Con Queen about certain films, I had been involved in. A few of the topics were very personal to me. The only people who would know about this, were the directors, producers, actors and stuntmen I have been associated with.

To lure me in, the Con Queen mentioned early on in our first conversation, that I was recommended by a few people within the film industry. There was one name he mentioned a producer from China, who I had worked for in Australia. I emailed her and she sent a message back, revealing she had never spoken with David or heard of him. The Con Queen got a lot of information to snare me from Facebook, Instagram and IMDB Pro. After that episode, I made sure I took down a lot of pictures and posts on Facebook and stopped accepting friend requests from people I didn't know.

Leigh arrived home after a couple of days and we hugged and embraced each other. We were so pleased to be back together. Some of our friends asked if I was okay. My phone started receiving calls and messages over the next few days. Nothing travels faster than light, except for bad news, which follows its own rules. One of our friends called Leigh one day, to say that I needed to let everyone know within our acting circle, that I had been ripped off. The funny thing was that it looks like I was one of the last guys in Asia to get hit by the scam. Many of them had been scammed, but none of them told anyone. Maybe they were too weak to tell anybody?

I was informed that some of them had engaged in sexual online activities with the Con Queen and doing all kinds of weird shit. Mirroring the attempts by Sarah Finn to coerce me into doing the same over the phone. Fearing the Con Queen would use the videos as blackmail, they refrained from coming forward. The lengths some people will go to, to achieve their dream of appearing in films are truly astonishing to me. So, lads, if you are reading this, you should have posted those videos on *Only Fans*, as you would have made more money! After finding out I had been stitched up, three actors and stuntmen contacted me, to tell me they had been ripped off which I appreciated.

Some of these guys, lost up to $20,000 and even travelled to Jakarta two times. It seems I got off lucky. It's a good thing my cash card didn't work! I only lost around $2,000. Thank God I wasn't stupid and resorted to violence, as I would have written this book in an Indonesian prison! In the film business, you get a lot of work through recommendations. I was even guilty of this myself by recommending my friend Frank, who was being groomed by the Con Queen. Frank nearly flew to Malaysia until I told him the whole thing was a scam. During my conversations with the Con Queen, I recommended two other people, but the Con Queen declined them both. They both were victims of this highly thought-out scam, but of course I didn't know it at the time. Later that afternoon, I received another call from an American Marine. I will keep his identity secret. He taught me a lot about firearms, from firing pistols to automatic weapons.

He is a good family man and friend. We have worked on many movies together. He told me some of his military friends, had been scammed too. The Con Queen manipulated some of the guys who had seen combat all over the world. The soldiers were banding together to hunt him down. They wanted as much information from me as possible. It seemed the Con Queen had the balls to rip off some pretty scary men, including MMA fighters and instructors. The Con Queen was very confident and untouchable, sitting behind his keyboard like a prick, just like those trolls you get on social media. Using psychological tactics to manipulate and intimidate people, he enjoyed playing with people's minds. I believe he thought he was a god. But when it comes down to it, he is nothing more than a parasite. A friend informed me that I needed to contact the FBI and K2 Intelligence. K2 Intelligence is a private investigation agency in the USA.

I contacted both organisations and wrote a statement about what had happened. I sent them copies of my emails and phone numbers so they could use them in their investigations. As an old saying goes, "Don't do the crime if you can't do the time." On the morning of November 26, 2020, police in the city of Manchester, England, arrested a man US officials believe to be the so-called Con Queen of Hollywood. Hargobind Tahilramani, a 41-year-old Indonesian convicted criminal, was arrested in downtown Manchester, ending many years of investigation by FBI and K2 intelligence agents. During his scamming career, Tahilramani allegedly passed himself off as several top male and female executives.

In 2017, he impersonated Amy Pascal, the Star Wars producer, Kathleen Kennedy and Paramount boss Sherry Lansing. He even duped some victims into believing he was Wendi Murdoch. One victim lost $70,000 to the scam. It is estimated that he made over one million dollars during his operation, ripping off hundreds of victims. If you Google his name, you will see his name plastered all over the internet. Tahilramani was raised in an affluent Jakarta neighbourhood. At the age of 18, he moved to the USA and attended college for two years. While in college, his dodgy dealings started and he was named in a lawsuit and accused of misappropriating school funds. In 2006, police in Jakarta arrested Tahilramani on charges of embezzlement and he spent six months in the notorious Cipinang Prison in Jakarta. It is estimated that his Con Queen scam started in 2012. In 2016, he set up shop in the UK, continuing to impersonate people and using his gang on the ground in Jakarta. Tahilramani has been charged with fraud and identity theft and more charges will be brought forward. The coconspirators on the ground in Jakarta have been identified.

To the best of my knowledge, he is held in a UK prison pending extradition to the United States. Human rights lawyers are defending him. They have tried to block his extradition to the USA because of his instability and mental condition. One physician indicated that Tahilramani believed he had been implanted with a microchip and heard voices. I don't believe that bullshit. He was trying to get the sympathy vote from the human rights brigade and playing them at their own game. I have no sympathy for the devil. Fingers crossed, some of his future prison inmates in America will regularly implant him with something else. Mind you, he might like that! One day, I do hope I will meet this paper tiger.

After this experience, I was very wary of people, especially in the film business. I even thought about giving up acting and didn't want anything to do with the film industry. I was so angry at the whole episode. It was the straw that broke the camel's back. Time heals and now my anger has faded and I put it down to life experience. I am more determined than ever to continue! It's like being wounded in battle the wound may heal, but the scars remain, serve as a reminder of the experience and make you stronger and more resilient. However, I am still suspicious of people and new producers who contact me directly and not through my agent. I am a very cautious person now and I check everyone out more than ever.

It is disheartening to hear that the authorities were only willing to investigate the Con Queen when high-profile individuals were involved. This suggests that the authorities prioritise the concerns of the wealthy and influential over those of ordinary citizens. It is important to remember that everyone deserves to be treated fairly by the justice system, regardless of their social status. The Con Queen's actions were harmful and should have been investigated regardless of who they affected. It is important to hold people accountable for their actions, regardless of the victim's identity. The authorities should have taken this case more seriously and pursued justice for all the victims. One law for them and another one for us. Some of the people I heard had to undergo trauma counselling after their ill-fated trips to Indonesia. This adventure was one of the biggest mistakes I have made in acting so far. I was blinded by the light. I thought I knew it all. How wrong was I? I was told the Con Queen tracked me for up to two years, gathering information on me all the time.

How many scammers create fake movie sets? I had never heard of it until I got scammed! I always remember the story of the 22 fake Apple stores in China that were so convincing that they even fooled their own staff! Remember, a positive mind finds opportunity in everything. A negative mind finds fault with everything. I have written about this small jaunt in this book, it's educated you and I have turned this nasty episode into something constructive. Making mistakes or being wrong is human. To admit those mistakes shows you have the ability to learn and grow wiser. I may not be perfect, but at least I am not fake. Remember that you can't trust everything you see. A word of warning to you all, remember, folks. When ambition gets out of hand, we are vulnerable to manipulation by others. Never trust everything you see. Even salt looks like sugar! Just before I close this crazy chapter, I had two authors from two well-known newspapers reach out to me about my adventures in Jakarta with The Hollywood Con Queen. Both asked for my full story. However, they didn't offer anything in return, not even a penny. I couldn't help but feel disappointed by their approach. It's not right for them to only benefit from my experience without giving anything back in return. I've encountered enough parasites in the entertainment industry leaching on others and this felt no different to me. You are in the same boat as the Con Queen. I truly believe that if you want something, you need to give a little back. It's a classic example of taking advantage of someone's ill-fated experience without consideration or gratitude. It's unfair and unethical. You are greedy bastards. The only people who benefit from the sale of their books are the author and the publication company's. For those of you who purchased my book, thank you so much! Part of the proceeds from this book will go to a charitable organisation. Fortunately, for those who didn't want to give something back, you've missed the glory of this story.

It Ain't All Glitz & Glamour

THE LAST TAKE

Merely seven days after returning from my trip to Indonesia, I found myself landing the lead role in an international commercial for a gambling site. Refusing to let the Con Queen bring me down, I gathered my strength and pressed forward with life. My persistence paid off as I started receiving offers for film roles once again. I was booked on two British gangster films, playing the main antagonist in a five-part movie series that would be filming in England and Portugal. I embraced this new challenge, knowing I would be pitted against a seasoned actor with an impressive resume, having worked alongside Stallone and earning nominations for two Primetime Emmy Awards, four Golden Globe Awards and two Screen Actors Guild Awards. The formidable opponent they chose for me was none other than Armand Assante, the notable actor famous for portraying the original John Gotti.

Rise of the Footsoldier Marbella was released and went down well with the public. The film's gritty portrayal of the Essex underworld resonated with audiences and my performance in the infamous fork scene with Pat Tate, played by Craig Fairbrass, went down well. I was inundated with positive feedback, with many fans praising my intensity and dedication to the role. The film's premiere events in both

It Ain't All Glitz & Glamour

Marbella and London were electrifying, showcasing the cult following that had emerged around the franchise. Fans eagerly approached me, complimenting my performance and expressing their fascination with the film's raw and authentic storytelling. The filmmakers at Carnaby International have masterfully crafted a series that captures the essence of the Essex underworld, captivating audiences worldwide. For me, it was a special moment to be in such an iconic British film. The *Footsoldier Marbella* premiere, however took an unexpected turn when an intoxicated individual disrupted the event. This incident, which has been discussed on various podcasts, initially led some audience members to believe it was a publicity stunt. However, the reality was far from staged.

The cast and crew had gathered for the film's premiere, ready to bask in the glow of their cinematic triumph. I found myself amidst a sea of familiar faces, the camaraderie of fellow actors and producers radiating through the air. Franky Lankester and his family, my partner Leigh and David Mahoney stood by my side as we navigated the throngs of eager photographers and journalists. Craig Fairbrass, Terry Stone, Nick Nevern, Emily Wyatt and the rest of the crew basked in the spotlight, their smiles reflecting the success of the film. The atmosphere was electric, a testament to the hard work and dedication that had brought this cinematic endeavour to life. Amidst the joyous celebration, a disquieting presence disrupted the harmony. A shadowy figure emerged from the crowd, his eyes glazed over and his movements erratic. An air of menace clung to him, casting a pall over the festivities. Muttering incoherently, the enigmatic figure weaved through the crowd, his presence casting a jarring note over the occasion. The Muppet walked through the crowd and was attempting to touch up some of the ladies. He made his way over to us and had his eyes on Frank's wife, Carina. He said something to Carina that was offensive and distasteful. The fool then made his way up to the stairs to the second floor of the building and he started hounding the owner of the film festival, Mac. Franky, ever the peacemaker, decided to intervene. He made his way upstairs to confront the individual. As he approached, he witnessed the man's abusive behaviour firsthand, his words laced with disrespect and aggression.

The tranquility of the Red Dog cinema was shattered by a sudden eruption of commotion from upstairs. The same disruptive individual who had caused unease earlier had resumed his disruptive conduct, this time targeting Mac. Franky, trained by the esteemed Martin Luna, a master of unarmed combat, possessed the skills to swiftly neutralise any threat. As the escalating commotion threatened to disrupt the premiere, Franky stepped forward, his demeanour calm and resolute. With a firm but polite voice, he requested the man's departure. However, the individual, powered by a sense of entitlement and intoxication, refused to comply. With the bottle, he attempted to strike Mac on the head and Frank saved Mac's skin by deflecting the bottle away. As the situation intensified, the agitated man lunged towards Franky, wielding the bottle. Franky's Krav-Maga training kicked in instinctively. With lightning-fast reflexes, he disarmed the individual, simultaneously delivering a strike that neutralised the threat. The crowd watched in awe as Franky, maintaining his composure, expertly defused the situation.

The disruptive individual's attempt to disrupt the harmonious atmosphere backfired spectacularly. His encounter with Franky, a fighting expert, served as a stark reminder of the consequences of his reckless behaviour. The unruly individual lost his footing in the ensuing scuffle and tumbled down the stairs. Frank told me he thought he had broken the guy's neck! Franky calmly descended the stairs, his composure unwavering amidst the chaos. With the individual subdued, Franky secured him in an arm lock and escorted the twat out of the venue, restoring order to the disrupted premiere.

Twenty minutes later, we were seated in the cinema. The anticipation for the film's premiere was abruptly shattered by the unexpected reappearance of the disruptive clown. This time, brandishing a menacing 12-inch kitchen knife, he stormed through the doors of the Red Dog cinema, his presence sending shock waves through the gathered crowd. The pre-show dialogue between Terry Stone and Andy Loveday was cut short as the individual's violent outburst disrupted the serene atmosphere. The security team and police, who were fortunately present at the venue, sprang into action, swiftly disarming the individual and apprehending him before he could inflict any harm. They carted him off to the cells and I believe he was prosecuted after. The funny thing about this whole episode was that some of the audience that night thought it was a publicity stunt.

My attendance at the *Footsoldier* premiere in London's East End, proved to be another eye-opening experience. The venue was packed with an enthusiastic subculture of *Footsoldier* enthusiasts, their devotion to the film was obvious and it was fascinating to witness such a passionate following for an independent production. As I waited at the reception, a man approached me, offering his congratulations on my performance in the fork scene. I couldn't recall his name, so I inquired about his origins. He responded, "I'm from Towie." Having spent many years living in Thailand, I was genuinely unaware of its existence. I politely asked, "Where's that, mate?" His response, laced with disbelief, was, "You don't know Towie?" My confusion was evident as I replied, "Is that near Southend?" His exasperated retort was, "Are you taking the piss?" I reiterated my genuine inquiry, "No, where is it?" His response was a huff as he walked away shaking his head pissed off. I suspect my lack of knowledge may have ruffled his ego. It wasn't until I spoke with Leigh that I discovered Towie was an acronym for *The Only Way is Essex,* a popular reality television show. You live and learn.

Following my return from the premier, I found myself once again in the vibrant country of Thailand. The bustling month of December saw the filming of the CBS TV series, *Blood and Treasure,* within its borders. However, amidst the excitement, a new virus, dubbed COVID, had emerged in China, causing a stir of panic within the production crew. As a result, the filming was abruptly halted and ultimately cancelled. Subsequently, all the actors were hastily flown back to their respective homes in the United States and Canada. Naively, I had believed that the situation would resolve itself within a few short weeks. Nevertheless, I had already been scheduled to film in England with the esteemed Armand, so within a matter of days, I took to the skies once again. During my return flight, I made a brief stop in Dubai. As I navigated through one of the departure gates, I couldn't help but notice that the Chinese passengers were being held in the main mall. I boarded my plane and settled into my seat. It was only then that I noticed a significant number of passengers sporting face masks. However, my attention was piqued when an odd couple walked by me, each wearing a full-face snorkel mask.

Upon my return to England, I found myself amidst the heightened security measures at the airport, with temperature scanners actively checking every individual. Quickly navigating through these protocols, I made my way to the film set in York. Working alongside Armand, an esteemed veteran in the movie industry, was an immense honour. Finally, here I was, playing a pivotal role as the main antagonist in a British gangster film. Immersed in the thrilling atmosphere of the film set, I couldn't help but reflect on how far I had come. However, the idyllic scenery soon gave way to a grim reality as the COVID-19 pandemic spread rapidly across the United Kingdom. The film I was working on with Armand was abruptly halted a week early as the entire world went into lockdown. Amidst the chaos and uncertainty, I was fortunate enough to secure a spot on the last train out of York before it was cancelled. Gazing out of the window, I couldn't help but feel a sense of disbelief as the world came to a standstill.

My plans to film on a project in Italy were swiftly

cancelled due to the pandemic and the entire film industry came to an abrupt halt. It closed down our dance business in Thailand and I had to get Leigh an emergency flight back to the UK. Faced with this predicament, I took decisive action and even managed to create a film during the lockdown period. Amidst all the chaos and uncertainty, I seized the opportunity to craft an exhilarating action movie, both in the UK and Thailand. Despite being physically separated; I directed my team via the internet and they courageously filmed in abandoned locations in Thailand. As for me, I ventured into the quiet solitude of farmer's fields and woods, undisturbed by human presence. One scene in the film required me to be run over, but without a stunt driver, I knew I had to devise a plan. In a moment of madness, I decided to run myself over while simultaneously driving the car, meticulously capturing it on film and utilising green screen techniques to achieve the desired effect. As you watch this scene, you will never suspect the ingenuity behind it. It goes to show that when faced with life's obstacles, we are truly capable of achieving the impossible.

After gracing the screen in many productions across the globe, I've had the privilege of encountering a remarkable array of individuals in the film industry. Along the way, I've formed genuine connections with some extraordinary people. I don't subscribe to the notion of placing actors on a pedestal. They're not superheroes or mythical creatures. Instead, I view them as fellow human beings, just like you and me. Hero worship holds no allure for me. I interact with them on an equal footing, treating them with the same respect and courtesy I extend to everyone else. In my eyes, true heroes are those who dedicate their lives to serving others. Doctors, nurses, first responders, soldiers and the like are the individuals who deserve our admiration and gratitude. Their selfless acts of courage and compassion make them exceptional individuals, truly deserving of the title "hero."

My journey in the action genre has led me down a path I never imagined I'd take. Life has a funny way of guiding us towards unexpected destinations. When I first started Muay Thai, I never dreamed it would lead me to Thailand, a country that ignited a deep passion within me. From Thailand, I ventured into the world of movies, embarking on a global adventure filled with exciting projects, from TV commercials to feature films. Along the way, I've encountered some incredible individuals who have enriched my life. I firmly believe in staying positive and embracing the twists and turns that life throws our way. Don't be afraid to step outside your comfort zone and explore new possibilities. While some people find comfort in a steady, traditional career, I encourage you to embrace your adventurous spirit and experience the world with an open mind. Of course, taking risks is an inevitable part of life. I've taken my fair share of chances, some that have paid off and others that have taught me valuable lessons. Just like any industry, the film world is a melting pot of personalities, both good and bad. While there are some exceptional individuals in the industry, there are also those who may not always align with your values.

As I reflect on my journey, I recognise that I've achieved many of the goals I set for myself. However, my passion for storytelling and exploration drives me to continue pursuing new challenges. Directing and producing my own films are also aspirations that I hold close to my heart. I believe that having control over the creative process would be incredibly rewarding. Additionally, I'm drawn to the world of documentaries, where I can delve into real-life stories and share them with audiences worldwide. While I'm still eager to explore acting opportunities, I'm also open to venturing beyond the action genre. After years of portraying tough, action-oriented characters, I'm ready to embrace roles that showcase a different side of my acting repertoire.

Embrace the journey, take risks and never stop learning. Life is a continuous adventure and I'm excited to see where the path takes me next. While the pampering and glamorous aspects of acting might get the spotlight, the reality for many actors is far from a holiday. The journey to landing roles, the constant struggle to stay relevant and the emotional rollercoaster of auditions and rejections can be incredibly challenging. Next time you watch a movie, check out the supporting actor's background in the film, you may be surprised where they came from. Some people might think I'm wealthy, I am but not in monetary terms. I am rich in memories.

The COVID-19 pandemic, though challenging, presented an unexpected blessing for three years. The global lockdown forced me to pause, reconnect with my family and rediscover my roots and I grew vegetables! I even embarked on a construction site job while things were quiet, a humbling experience that grounded me. Eager to reignite my passion for filmmaking, I'm diving back into the industry with renewed vigour. I'm also planning to write a series of books, including a collection of action-packed stories. With plenty of untold tales still left to unveil, my debut book has barely scratched the surface of my experiences. Therefore, I am thrilled to announce I am writing my second book. *"It Ain't All Glitz and Glamour, Part 2, The Untold Stories."*

This upcoming installment will feature many stories that I couldn't fit into this book. It covers working with action icons, successes, filming on amazing sets, stalkers and getting blown off my feet and burned in an action sequence gone wrong. One chapter delves into the behind-the-scenes of the indie film *English Dogs* and the unexpected consequences that followed working with Crazy Dave Blazejko.

Little did I know that his involvement in this project would thrust me into the limelight and that I would nearly face prosecution as a kingpin in one of Australia's largest illegal commercial steroid operations. The manuscript *Bareknuckle* is slated to transform into both a documentary and a publication. I hope you've enjoyed my book and spat out a biscuit here and there, on some of my stories. I've now worked on more than 70 productions and I still have a few wild tales to share. As a regular geezer well, kind of working in the film business, I've discovered that the key to success is making your own opportunities.

So, my fellow adventurers who dared to crack open this book! I would like to sincerely thank you for your support. I'll tell you a secret. Nobody truly knows what they're doing in life. We're all just winging it in this cosmic improv show. So,

embrace the awkwardness, celebrate the stumbles and chase those crazy dreams like a squirrel after an acorn. You've got nothing to lose. Now go out there and paint the world with your unique brand of awesomeness. If you have ambition, just go for it. I truly salute you!
But remember,
"It Ain't All Glitz and Glamour."

It Ain't All Glitz & Glamour

DISCLAIMER

The names and identifying characteristics of some individuals have been changed. This book was written by memory and mine is imperfect. I've done my best to be faithful to my experiences and when possible, have consulted others who were also present during that time. I the author in no way represents any company, corporation, or brand, mentioned herein. The views expressed in this memoir are solely those of me the author. Although I the author has made every effort to ensure that the information in this book was correct at press time, I does not assume and hereby disclaims any liability to any party for any loss, damage, or disruption caused by errors or omissions, whether such errors or omissions result from negligence, accident, or any other cause.

www.ingramcontent.com/pod-product-compliance
Lightning Source LLC
Chambersburg PA
CBHW052133070526
44585CB00017B/1813